STYLE

TO ACHIEVE STYLE,

BEGIN BY AFFECTING NONE.

—William Strunk, Jr., and E. B. White,
The Elements of Style

SIMON & SCHUSTER
NEW YORK   LONDON   TORONTO   SYDNEY

always gracious,
sometimes irreverent

STYLE

BY

Kate Spade

edited by Ruth Peltason and Julia Leach
illustrations by Virginia Johnson

Labor Day has officially arrived, so does that mean you can no longer wear white? What seasonal rules, if any, still apply?

Wearing white is a personal preference, and you needn't be bound by long-standing traditions. If white is basic to your wardrobe, then by all means wear it year-round. The trick is to tweak it so that it looks natural to each season. In early fall, try an ivory-and-blue seersucker blazer with a scarf. It's the perfect follow-up to the pure white of summer.

Even though you love shirting stripes, some vertical stripes are a bit too preppy for your taste. Is there a stripe that's a little dressier and has more poise?

Nothing's classier than a stripe, but that shouldn't limit you to more conventional patterns. Used horizontally, a wide stripe has graphic impact. For a more subtle and less-expected style, a diagonal stripe instantly energizes a shirt and removes it from any boarding-school associations.

You have limited storage space, yet no matter how many times you decide to weed your closet you can't bring yourself to give away some sentimental favorites, such as figure skates you haven't worn since you were ten. Are you lacking the "clean" gene?

The answer is simple, with no apologies required: some things are "forever clothes" and their sentimental meaning gives them the right to remain in your closet. But it might be a good idea to put them neatly on an out-of-the-way shelf.

HAVE YOU EVER WONDERED...?

You have a perfectly good dress for evening, but admittedly it's a bit on the plain side. How can you look more spruced up?

Accessorize, accessorize, accessorize. Nothing elevates something simple like a necklace of brightly colored stones or shoes with a lot of lift and sparkle. It's what you add that gives personality and style to your appearance.

At the better vintage shops, cashmere sweaters and party dresses are always in such good condition. How can you keep the same standards at home?

Whether clothing is vintage or new, fine garments should always be hung on padded hangers—wire doesn't have enough support. Take special care when it comes to cleaning. Cashmere, for instance, should always be washed by hand in mild detergent and rinsed well. That's what our grandmothers did, and that's why their sweaters look so good today.

Most of the time you carry a fairly utilitarian bag—generously sized and neutral in color. But you're going to a cocktail party after work and would like something that's more fun and that doesn't scream "business." What are your options?

Fortunately, you don't have to sacrifice your day needs for evening festivities. Use your large bag for work, and in it take a small bag for later. A brightly colored box-shaped purse easily slips over your wrist so you can enjoy a cocktail and hors d'oeuvre without spilling one or dropping the other.

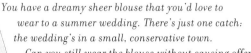

You have a dreamy sheer blouse that you'd love to wear to a summer wedding. There's just one catch: the wedding's in a small, conservative town. Can you still wear the blouse without causing offense?

You are right to consider the feelings of others, especially at a wedding. Wear a pretty camisole under your blouse, which will add a layer of color as well as a layer of "protection."

Every time you pack for a trip, invariably your blouses crinkle or your pants get crease marks in the wrong places. Since you don't have room to take a steam iron, what are some packing tips?

Tissue paper is a traveler's best friend. For very special garments, you can begin by placing some tissue in the corners of your suitcase. Otherwise, wrap your things in tissue and use flat sheets of tissue between layers. Plastic dry-cleaning bags are also helpful, but unlike tissue paper they will cause your things to shift and slide.

In recent years you've worked for yourself, but you've just accepted a position with a good-sized company in a creative industry. Does this mean you need to change your casual wardrobe?

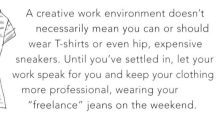

A creative work environment doesn't necessarily mean you can or should wear T-shirts or even hip, expensive sneakers. Until you've settled in, let your work speak for you and keep your clothing more professional, wearing your "freelance" jeans on the weekend.

After months of working out, you finally have a flat stomach and slim hips that you'd like to show off. Are many places or events taboo for your new belly-button outfits?

Common sense can answer most of your concerns, but unless you're seventeen or on familiar turf, a bit of cover-up is a no-fail course to follow. Sometimes what you can't see (but can only imagine) is far more revealing.

Real pearls are costly, yet you adore them. Is it all right to mix fine jewelry with costume?

Wearing jewelry with style is about considering shape, color, and proportion. If your grandmother's pearl necklace is perfection with your costume Dior pearl brooch, then wear them together often. Make them a signature look all your own.

Your sister loves things like scarves and gloves, but her taste tends toward neutral tones and plain styles. You'd love her to have something that's a bit livelier. What's fun but not too wild?

Consider a gift of brightly colored two-tone suede gloves. The two-tone look is classic (think of the black-and-tan Chanel pumps) and colors such as turquoise or deep pink add a splash of color to a black or brown coat.

And in conclusion, have you ever wondered if you didn't have clothes on whether you would still have style?

"The finest clothing made is a person's skin, but, of course society demands something more than this."

—Mark Twain

CONTENTS

STYLE, FROM SCHIAPARELLI
TO STRUNK & WHITE

"Fashion changes ... style remains."
—*Diana Vreeland*

Living in New York can be the most liberating place in the world, especially when it comes to the business of fashion. Style is abundant in New York—it's in the buildings and in the parks, it's the way flowers are displayed on nearly every corner, it's the fact that art and music are concentrated here, and it's where people who love books and movies talk about them all the time. It's a city where style is, quite simply, in the air. In my travels, I see style everywhere, from Mexico to Napa Valley to Tokyo.

Maybe someone like Diana Vreeland was born with style, or Grace Kelly, who surely was born with beauty and style. I was born in the Midwest, and style wasn't much on anyone's mind. If style meant anything in my early years, it meant figuring out a way to look different from my four sisters, which was quite a challenge. I used to rummage around old thrift shops when I was a teenager, and I still shop little vintage stores wherever I am. I've always loved strong, saturated color, when I was fourteen and now even more so.

I've never had a style mentor in the conventional sense; for me, photographs and movies have always been my source of inspiration. When I consider how stylish Jean Seberg looked in *Bonjour Tristesse,* or how Jane Fonda in *Barefoot in the Park* personified the vivaciousness of a newlywed, I feel inspired. When Katharine Hepburn wore trousers it wasn't about rebellion, it was about finding what made her feel most herself. By finding her "center of gravity," she made trousers look chic.

My husband, Andy, likes to say that style is innate. He and I both feel that style is the sum of so many things—beginning with a sense of who you are and having self-confidence. It's about getting the most mileage out of what works best on you. I'm a firm believer in wearing what makes you happy. And the only rules I'd encourage anyone to follow are their own rules. (If Chanel or Schiaparelli had followed the prevailing notions of their day, would we have the black jersey dress or shocking pink?)

In this book, neither Andy nor I have any magic formulas to offer about having style, but I can tell you that true style comes from opening yourself to the world around you—to books and movies, to art, to music and travel, and especially to other people. Furthermore, style is what the writers William Strunk and E. B. White called *clarity*.

I could never portray myself as a style guru, but there are plenty of women whose style I admire, from Babe Paley to Björk, and their impressive achievements are mentioned here. My particular inspirations and loves are included, beginning with a large section devoted to the colors I most adore and ways of combining them. And since I would gladly wear the same pants seven days in a row as long as I could change my accessories at will (they're really the backbone of my wardrobe), you'll find ideas for shoes, handbags, hats, and jewelry. (For instance, I love wearing a stack of sparkly bracelets or one big, chunky necklace.) Style in the office, party style, and especially play style (going to the beach, riding a bike, even lazing in a hammock) are all featured here. The last section draws attention to maintaining style—organizing your closet, taking care of vintage clothes, and tips on keeping cashmere and jewelry in good condition.

I've often thought that Diana Vreeland's "why don't you...?" columns were pure genius. For me, they're little gifts because in their special way they liberated how a woman thought about herself and the world around her. Their magic lay in the freedom of choice and creativity they offered. In a much more humble way, I hope that *Style* will offer ideas and kindle a fresh sense of spirit and adventure. Style is a little like mercury: try to put your finger on it and it moves.

Kate Spade
New York City, 2003

SECTION ONE

Style and the World

Finding Style in All the Right Places

Books · Movies · Art

Design/Architecture · Tradition/Modernism

Kate On Style: A Work in Progress

Think Pink · Pattern Crazy

Achieving Your Style and Letting Go of Style

FINDING STYLE IN ALL THE RIGHT PLACES

"I think it's nice if you tell people that you've been inspired by other people or by books or movies, because sometimes it's intimidating to think that if you don't have the idea yourself you aren't truly creative or unique. I've never thought of style as something you invent, like trying to come up with the proverbial better mousetrap. I think that style is part of the way we live, so it makes perfect sense to me to keep an open mind and explore. Then you can adapt what you've learned and call it your own. That seems fair to me."

BOOKS

Dr. Seuss, Winnie-the-Pooh, or Beatrix Potter are the first magical stepping stones into the world of words. From there it's a quick leap into the deeper waters of rebellion, romance, and adventure (think *Catcher in the Rye* and *Tender is the Night*). Want to learn witty repartee? Read Jane Austen. Bask in the sidelines of privilege? Open up to any page in *A Wonderful Time*, by Slim Aarons. Toy with trouble? *The Big Sleep* delivers it in spades. And if you're not sure what you like or who you are, just repeat, "I am Sam I am."

MOVIES

Movies are the perfect road for time travel. If you want to look at hair, makeup, and dress, watch Jacques Demy's *Umbrellas of Cherbourg* (coiffed and ultra matchy-matchy) and Woody Allen's *Annie Hall* (loose—both the hair and the clothes). Or if family values are your interest, consider the changes in the American family: there's Orson Welles's *The Magnificent Ambersons* (uptight and mired in the past) and Wes Anderson's *The Royal Tenenbaums* (freewheeling and then some). Movies are the ultimate in entertainment, education, and inspiration.

"ART, LITERATURE, ENTERTAINMENT, TRAVEL, POLITICS, DÉCOR, FOOD, AND DRESS ARE EXPRESSIONS OF EVERYDAY LIVING AND OF COMMON INTEREST TO MEN AND WOMEN ALIKE."

—FLEUR COWLES, *FLAIR*

ART

Here the message and the experience are purely visual and entirely personal. Stand with a friend in front of paintings by Diebenkorn and Rothko. Then describe the paintings to each other. With another friend stand in front of a photograph by Robert Frank. Again, describe the image. Spend an afternoon going to art galleries and museums, where you live and also when you travel. Art is an international language, and when the art begins "talking" to you, inspiration strikes.

DESIGN/ARCHITECTURE

Your morning coffee cup, the chair you sit on, even the sunglasses you wear, all say something about your style. No matter where you live—in rodeo country or surrounded by skyscrapers—inspiration is always at hand. The flourishes in a Beaux-Arts building might express pure beauty to you; for someone else, the glass skin of modern architecture is a high note of clarity and precision.

TRADITION/MODERNISM

Consider a pair of Keds, with their ubiquitous little blue rubber label on the back of the shoe, their pebbly underfoot, softly thick laces. Simple perfection in a size 7. Then there is the Puma walking shoe, with its state-of-the art air mesh fabric, its ergonomically correct sole support, its hip Velcro closures. Twenty-first-century perfection in a size 7. Again and again, the choice—and the blend—of tradition and modernism is yours. Why not listen to Ella Fitzgerald on your iPod?

BOOKS

"I can't imagine my life or my bedside table without books. It seems that Andy and I are always picking up photography and art books, or just snooping around new and used book shops wherever we are. I tend to go for big picture books, whereas Andy always manages to pluck out some quirky book—his latest find is a paperback from 1950 called *Popularity Plus*. I don't know if you can judge a book by its cover, but you can tell a lot about people by their home library."

BOOKS THAT INSPIRE AND FILL THE WORLD WITH THOUGHT AND VISION . . .

Anything by
Beatrix Potter

Goodbye Picasso by David Douglas Duncan
("An homage to Picasso—so intimate.")

The Elements of Style by William Strunk, Jr., and E. B. White
("My husband's favorite book.")

Allure by Diana Vreeland

Tiffany's Table Manners for Teen-Agers by Thomas Hoving
("Certainly the best and the funniest book on kids and manners. I love Joe Eula's drawings.")

The Americans by Robert Frank

The Sun Also Rises by Ernest Hemingway

Then by Alexander Lieberman

Observations by Truman Capote and Richard Avedon
("Hard to find, especially still in its original slipcase.")

A Wonderful Time by Slim Aarons
("The ultimate in stylish living.")

Etiquette by Emily Post ("Indispensable.")

The Big Sleep by Raymond Chandler

The Jump Book by Philippe Halsman

Sparkle and Spin: A Book About Words by Paul Rand

Cowboy Kate
by Sam Haskins

The In and Out Book by Robert Benton and Harvey Schmidt ("Pure pleasure—and so true!")

"My personal recommendation is a book that Andy made by photocopying book covers, which he titled *An Argument for Looking At Books Instead of Reading Them*."

The quick brown fox jumps over a lazy dog.

ENDURING STYLE...
BASKERVILLE TYPEFACE (C. 1750s)

John Baskerville was something of a perfectionist, giving
six years of artisanal attention to creating this typeface.
The Baskerville face is distinguished for its rounded
characters, the contrast between its thick and thin lines,
and exquisitely fine serifs. It's a traditional face, naturally
versatile, and used customarily for book text. The face
fell into disuse sometime in the 1800s but was revived
by the Monotype Corporation in the early 1900s.
By 1923, it had become a favorite among book designers.

WRITERS WE READ AGAIN AND AGAIN...

John Cheever

David Sedaris

James Thurber

Mark Twain

J. D. Salinger

Henry David Thoreau

Jane Austen

W. Somerset Maugham

F. Scott Fitzgerald

Dawn Powell

William Faulkner

James Salter

Glenn O'Brien

The quick brown fox jumps over a lazy dog.

ENDURING STYLE...
FUTURA TYPEFACE (1927)

In contrast to the delicate serifs of Baskerville, the sans
serif Futura is about bold geometric and symmetrical forms.
Futura, designed by the German Paul Renner, has its roots
in the Bauhaus and De Stijl art movements. Then, as
now, Futura embraces a modernist ethos, making it
among the most classically modern typefaces used today.

WHY THE QUICK BROWN FOX?

Traditionally, typefaces are displayed using the sentence "The quick brown fox jumps
over a lazy dog." That's because this is a pangram, a sentence that contains all the
letters of the alphabet. Other oddball pangrams include: "Back in my quaint garden
jaunty zinnias vie with flaunting phlox"; "Fred specialized in the job of making
very quaint wax toys"; and "Viewing quizzical abstracts mixed up hefty jocks."

MOVIES

"My favorite nights are when Andy and I are at home with a stack of movies to watch. I love movies where the clothes and the 'look' of the film are especially pronounced, as in *Bonnie and Clyde*. I know it's a gangster film, but when you see it you're really watching Faye Dunaway and Warren Beatty. There she is in some dusty Texas town during the Depression, but she's so stylish you wonder whether she hasn't been sneaking a look at Italian *Vogue*. That's the magic of film—the leap of faith the viewer takes. The styling of a film—how it looks, what the colors are like, and how it speaks to you personally—is what Andy calls 'selective perception,' and I think he's right. Or at least, that's part of the style we look for in movies."

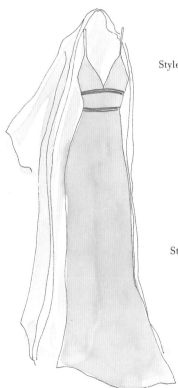

STYLE 101

Style in Cahoots—*Bonnie and Clyde*

Style in Space—*Barbarella, 2001: A Space Odyssey, Star Trek* films

Style in the Bush—*Out of Africa, The African Queen*

Style in Debt—*Mildred Pierce*

Style on a Boat—*Purple Noon*

Style on the Road—*Easy Rider, Paper Moon*

Style by the Pool—*High Society, Sexy Beast*

Style at the Bar—*Butterfield 8, Klute*

Style at School—*The Group, To Sir with Love*

Style on the Beach—*Bonjour Tristesse*

Style in the City—*Barefoot in the Park, The Best of Everything*

Style in the Courtroom—*To Kill a Mockingbird*

Style in the Rain—*Singin' in the Rain*

Grace Kelly described herself as looking "like a peach parfait" in the negligee designed for her by Edith Head in Hitchcock's *Rear Window*.

MOVIES WITH STYLE...

Ninotchka (Ernst Lubitsch, 1939)
Adrian called his adaptation of Schiaparelli's "Breton sailor" a "little bit of a hat—
a crazy little hat." On Garbo the hat is oddly alluring.

Le Ballon Rouge (Albert Lamorisse, 1956)
Never did the color red have such heart and embrace such hope.

Goldfinger (Guy Hamilton, 1964)
For the title credits and musical score that still thrills,
as does all that gold paint.

Umbrellas of Cherbourg (Jacques Demy, 1964)
Pourquoi pas? Why shouldn't interiors and clothes match?

Bonnie and Clyde (Arthur Penn, 1967)
Faye Dunaway gives the beret an American facelift.

The Graduate (Mike Nichols, 1967)
Anne Bancroft's tiger-striped hair and leopard
coat say it all.

The Swimmer (Frank Perry, 1968)
Except for Burt Lancaster, everyone and everything swings in this gimlet-eyed
portrait of pre-hippie America: seeing Joan Rivers in a hot pink V-neck fringed
with chromium yellow and white beads packs high-intensity voltage.

Two for the Road (Stanley Donen, 1967)
Audrey Hepburn, the perennial "good girl" of film, goes mod in Mary Quant,
Hardy Amies, Paco Rabanne, and Courrèges.

Annie Hall (Woody Allen, 1977)
Diane Keaton wears Ralph Lauren, all of it a size too big.

The Royal Tenenbaums (Wes Anderson, 2001)
The little hair clips. The smoky eyes. The old fur coat. Gwyneth Paltrow
personifies tattered elegance.

"SHOW BUSINESS IS DOG EAT DOG.
IT'S WORSE THAN DOG EAT DOG.
IT'S DOG DOESN'T RETURN DOG'S PHONE CALLS."

—WOODY ALLEN, FROM *CRIMES AND MISDEMEANORS*

MOVIES THAT MAKE US WANT TO LOOK AND DRESS AND *FEEL* A CERTAIN WAY...

Athletic, like Katharine Hepburn in her high-fitting trousers or little tennis skirt in *Pat and Mike*

Daring, like Charlotte Rampling in *Georgy Girl*

Sophisticated, like Catherine Deneuve in *The Last Metro*

In love, like Anouk Aimée in *A Man and a Woman*

Collegiate, like Ali MacGraw in *Love Story*

FILM DIRECTORS I ADMIRE...

Mike Nichols	Preston Sturgess
Jacques Tati	François Truffaut
Woody Allen	Orson Welles
Spike Jonze	Wes Anderson
Sofia Coppola	Albert Brooks
Jean-Luc Goddard	P. T. Anderson
Blake Edwards	Billy Wilder

AND A GRATEFUL NOD TO COSTUME DESIGNERS...

Adrian (*The Women, Philadelphia Story*)

Edith Head (*All About Eve, The Sting*)

Mary Quant (*Two for the Road, Georgy Girl*)

Irene Sharaff (*Cleopatra*)

Anna Hill Johnstone (*The Swimmer, Alice's Restaurant*)

Orry-Kelly (*Irma la Douce, Gypsy*)

Karen Patch (*Rushmore, The Royal Tenenbaums*)

Hubert de Givenchy (*Funny Face, Charade*)

Phyllis Dalton (*Doctor Zhivago, Lawrence of Arabia, Dead Again*)

ART

"When we were growing up, to me art meant paintings by artists such as Leroy Neiman or, for Andy, Farrah Fawcett posters. Nowadays, I'm drawn to old drawings and portraits, and Andy goes for contemporary photography and odd, conceptual works. Usually, though, we buy each other art as gifts and that keeps the mix in our house lively and unpredictable."

ARTISTS I ADMIRE . . .

Early Milton Avery	Sonia Delauney
Irving Penn	Mark Rothko
Richard Diebenkorn	Pablo Picasso
Grandma Moses	Alexander Calder
John Currin	Joan Miró
Donald Baechler	Will Cotton
Ellsworth Kelly	Lee Friedlander
Andy Warhol	Elliott Erwitt
Agnes Martin	Piet Mondrian
Tina Barney	Louise Dahl-Wolfe
Lisa Yuskavage	Rene Ricard
Eric Fischl	Diane Arbus
Robert Frank	Gerhard Richter
Peter Halley	Maurizio Cattelan
Larry Sultan	Edward Hopper
Cy Twombly	Norman Rockwell
Jean-Michael Basquiat	

Josef Albers

classic nude

Jasper Johns

Yves Saint Laurent's Mondrian dress appeared in 1965.

DESIGN/ARCHITECTURE

"Until I was in my twenties, I didn't give much thought to 'things' around me.
Now I can't imagine not caring about the shape of a chair or the design of a vase,
even the paving stones on our patio. I think good citizenship includes a healthy
regard for design, though I do believe it's only fair to have your likes and dislikes."

PEOPLE, PLACES, THINGS

New England saltbox

Le Corbusier

Mies van der Rohe

Beach shack

Alexander Girard

The Glass House

Bauhaus

Shaker table

Federal style

Tibor and Maira Kalman

Eliel Saarinen

Greene and Greene

Coney Island roller coaster

Charles and Ray Eames

Saul Bass

Eileen Gray

Jean Prouvé chairs,
c. 1950

"YOU SHOULDN'T TALK
ABOUT ART, YOU SHOULD DO
IT. I'M A COMMENTATOR.
I'M AN EXCITER-UPPER.
I'M A SNIFFER-AROUNDER."

—PHILIP JOHNSON

Frank Lloyd Wright's Fallingwater

Teepee

ENDURING STYLE...
THE SLINKY (1943)

Its birth was an accident, but its appeal has been long-lasting.
Since a mechanical engineer first knocked the steel spring
off his desk, the many-ringed wonder of clean design
and simplicity has delighted generations of children and
adults for its elasticity and buoyant feeling in the hand.

TRADITION/MODERNISM

"Even if you're traditional, you shouldn't be afraid of being modern. What's interesting is combining the two sensibilities. When fused, a third, unique aesthetic is expressed."

School clock · George Nelson Eye Clock

Monticello · The Rothko Chapel

Royal Worcester porcelain bowl · Alvar Aalto "wave" vase

The Louvre · Guggenheim Bilbao

Typewriter · iMac

Chippendale chair · Swan Chair by Arne Jacobsen

Edith Wharton · Raymond Carver

Floral circle skirt · Geoffrey Beene dress—black jersey and white-hammered satin

Casablanca · *Contempt*

1973 Impala station wagon · 1973 BMW 2002

Strand of pearls · Strand of pearls ("Pearls defy categorization. The effect is in how you wear them.")

"Without tradition, art is a flock of sheep without a shepherd."
—Winston Churchill

"You are born modern. You do not become so."
—Jean Baudrillard

KATE ON STYLE:
A WORK IN PROGRESS

"When you are defining your own style, it's so important not to be nervous. Part of style is confidence—you need to own your sense of style and be relaxed. If you've already pulled off a simple, clean look, then you can add just one great piece: shoes or a brooch. Find something you're drawn to, something you can't stop thinking about. Enjoy it. Play. I'm a big proponent of owning pieces that you cannot wait to wear. You want to find something that speaks to you in a totally personal way."

"DRESS BY YOUR *OWN* RULES. STYLE IS NOT ABOUT *THE* RULES."

"STRIPES are one of the strongest graphic patterns I can think of. This linen coat is ideal for spring and summer. The coat is like a great beach umbrella."

"Little by little I've been collecting these bracelets, and I love wearing them together, regardless of whether the colors match my clothes, or their noise makes my dog bark."

"Love at first sight—when I saw this skirt, which I think was from one of Tom Ford's first collections for Gucci, I thought to myself, 'I have to have it.' It's so wonderfully bright and full, and who can resist oranges?"

"My mother was a freak for SUNGLASSES. She even had drawers just for her sunglasses in the family breakfront in our dining room."

"YOU CAN LEARN HOW TO TIE A SHOE.
YOU CAN LEARN HOW TO REBUILD AN ENGINE.
YOU CAN LEARN HOW TO SPEAK SWAHILI WITH A FRENCH ACCENT.
BUT STYLE IS INNATE."

—ANDY SPADE

"I'm pretty consistent about some things, and WICKER is one of them. I like just about anything wicker, whether it's a chair, a picnic hamper, or a handbag. The proportions of this purse are modern, but the result (in part because of the wicker) is timeless."

"I don't feel that you *can't* wear white after Labor Day, but if I were to, the outfit would have to be pretty exceptional . . . such as a vintage dress by Courrèges."

"SOMEWHERE IN BETWEEN IS HOW I DRESS."

"Everything that Alpana Bawa designs says COLOR and this scarf is like a row of oversized lifesavers. I like the fact that Alpana Bawa's colors are never ordinary and always so saturated."

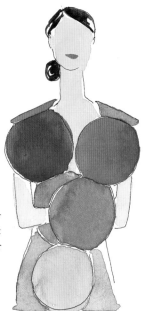

"I LIKE COATS THAT ARE BELTED—A LITTLE DEFINITION AT THE WAIST MAKES AN OUTFIT MORE FEMININE, ESPECIALLY FOR SOMETHING DRESSY."

"A perfect example of something that's strong but not loud—to me, there's a huge difference. This John Anthony coat is double-faced satin, which feels incredible, and it's reversible. The DEEP YELLOW YOKE is pure luxury."

"STYLE CAN'T BE PURCHASED."

—ANDY SPADE

"We all have our indulgences, and I confess that this Dolce & Gabbana duster was one of mine. The PROPORTIONS work for me: I like my sleeves on the short side, which is great for all the bracelets I'm always wearing, and the three-quarter length is ideal with a pair of black cigarette pants and high heels. I tend to wear coats indoors the way other people wear sweaters, so it's not unusual for me to keep this on all day or evening."

"It probably seems a little unconventional, but I really do use PENCIL CASES as evening bags. I like that they're small and have such a compact design."

NO ANTLERS, NOT EVER

"I can usually tell when a wife has dressed her husband, and there's a part of me that thinks, 'Let him dress his own way.' It's great to suggest things, but don't *dress* a man. You really want to avoid dressing up your husband like he's a Christmas package. I always felt a little sorry for the guy wearing the silly reindeer sweater that matches his wife's. You know that wasn't his idea."

—Andy Spade

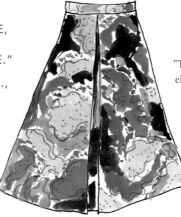

"I DON'T BUY A LOT OF BASICS. WHEN I SHOP FOR BLACK PANTS, I'M LIKELY TO COME HOME WITH A SCARF AND PINK SHOES."

"I've worn this hat made by Philip Treacy for years, and I never tire of it, which is a sign of its inherent 'rightness.' It's a hat with a mind of its own."

"AVOID THE ELABORATE, THE PRETENTIOUS, THE COY, AND THE CUTE."

—WILLLIAM STRUNK, JR., AND E.B. WHITE

"This skirt is perfect with a chocolate sweater. The fabric is VINTAGE and the designer, Barbara Tfank, is amazing at working one-of-a-kind fabrics into modern silhouettes."

"I think everyone should have a favorite pair of loafers, and these HOUNDSTOOTH flats are perfect for me. The thin red piping is a little wink of color that takes them from being ordinary to something special."

SINGULAR STYLE

Diana Vreeland—"Style always seemed so instinctual to her."

Katharine Hepburn—"She painted her nails red and I like that about her. Besides, she made trousers seem so chic."

Björk—"I admire her for her utterly singular approach to everything. She's so brave."

Lauren Hutton—"Lauren Hutton has such a genuine look. And I don't think she has to work at it, either."

Betty Parsons—"Here's a remarkable woman who had the courage to open her own gallery just after World War II. No wonder *ARTnews* called her 'the den mother of Abstract Expressionism.'"

"Absolutely one of my better vintage finds. Although this CHINOISERIE coat came with a beige-colored strapless dress, I tend to put it with something simple, such as black or white pants."

"WHEN I WANT TO ADD DRAMA TO A COAT, I SWEEP UP THE COLLAR AND CLOSE IT WITH A BROOCH."

With her natural beauty and gap-toothed smile, Lauren Hutton was the highest-paid model on the circuit in 1973.

"I'm not big into full shoes. I guess I prefer slingbacks because I wear them year-round, always without stockings. I love a LIGHTNESS to the shoe, something pretty or elegant."

THINK PINK

"Sometimes you have to be creative with color. Some years ago in the fall, I had on a gray sweater, a pink jacket, and a green scarf, as well as a pair of black pants. The jacket was bouclé, and I admit the fabric helped make the color combination less in-your-face, but the point is that you can be unafraid to mate soft and strong colors, if that's what makes you happy."

"Bright color makes you feel so good. You feel prettier. Much as I like color, I never like if it becomes kitschy. When Vera made scarves, there was nothing cutesy about them. They always made you feel happy, which is also true of Bonnie Cashin—her shapes and colors are always so clean. I think it's important to remember that bright color and pattern can be very sophisticated and make you look strong."

"I LIKE ACCENTING PINK WITH ORANGE. AND GREEN WITH PINK AND WHITE."

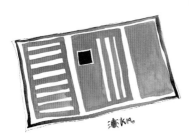

VERA, THE LADYBUG LADY
Those little telltale ladybugs owe their origin to the silk-screened botanical shapes that Vera Neumann first put onto place mats in the 1940s. She remains loved for her exuberantly colored designs (florals, geometrics, dots, and stripes), which were inspired by her studio in the country. As for the ladybug— Vera regarded it as a symbol of good luck.

Bonnie Cashin, doubleknit jersey and avocado-green suede dress, 1973

"When I read Diana Vreeland's 'why don't you' suggestions, I find that she has so many clever ideas. I'm continually inspired by her original thoughts. What would fashion have been like without her?"

WHY DON'T YOU...
BY DIANA VREELAND

Wear violet mittens with everything?

Travel with a little raspberry-colored cashmere blanket to throw over yourself in hotels and trains?

Try the lovely combination of tourmalines and pink rubies?

Tie black tulle bows on your wrists?

Color as design: Alexander Girard's iconic logo on the menu for the restaurant La Fonda del Sol, in New York, c. 1960

THE ART OF THE SELECTION

Color is the most disarming seduction: you might love yellow, but if your skin is more olive than pink, then yellow on you is like a light flashing "caution, caution." Light and dark (black + white), warm and cool (watermelon + navy), monochrome (chocolate brown + taupe + white), or medley (white + green + pink + turquoise) are all in the art of the selection.

GREEN

"I can't imagine a day without green—for me, this is the most basic of colors, a neutral I turn to again and again. Much as I love green with white, black, or pink, I think it's great combined with all three colors—then it has real poise. And of course certain shades of green with blue are heavenly, such as kelly green and turquoise, a combination that always makes me smile."

From the vibrant hues of springtime to Van Eyck's *Arnolfini* bridal gown, green means freshness, youth, and fertility. As the most restful color in the spectrum, green evokes the safety of traffic lights, the calm of nature, and Kermit's easy grin.

COMBINATIONS

green + **AQUA**

green + **WHITE**

green + **CORAL**

In *Bonjour Tristesse*, Elsa wears an emerald green dress with a coral sash when she dances the merengue through the streets of Saint-Tropez.

The swimming pool colors of aqua and green are among the most soothing color combinations.

Green suede gloves peeking out from under the sleeves of a fitted riding jacket.

Picking up your aunt at the airport in olive green leather pumps and a camel hair coat.

Easter lunch in a kelly green silk tunic and Ted Muehling jeweled earrings.

Muehling's earrings (and his silver tea strainer) were inspired by Queen Anne's lace.

For the Orchid Ball, wear a softly ruffled silk taffeta dress, made by Jeanne Lanvin, c. 1930.

Dr. Seuss wrote *Green Eggs and Ham* after his editor dared him to write a book using fewer than fifty different words.

WEAR-ANYWHERE WELLINGTONS

PINK

"I like pink when it's strong. I never want color to be cute, especially pink, which is one reason I steer clear of pale pink. For me, a deep raspberry pink works best, and then it seems grown-up."

Mix red and white—passion and purity—to make pink, the most feminine of hues. The signature color of romance, pink also signifies friendship, tranquility, and honor.

HOW ABOUT...

A watermelon-pink raincoat to brighten up a damp April day.

A pink beaded evening gown for a grand party, similar to the one that Jackie Onassis wore to the opening of the Mona Lisa exhibit at the National Gallery of Art, in 1963.

A pink Vera silk scarf tied loosely in your hair—perfect with white jeans, a white T-shirt, and a 1967 Schwinn bicycle.

In *Funny Face*, Kay Thompson as a fashion magazine editor (based on Diana Vreeland) is captivated by a swatch of pink cloth and encourages her staff and women across the nation to "Banish black! Down to the kitchen sink, think pink!"

EVEN PANTIES ARE BEST
WHEN THEY'RE PINK.

WOULD WE HAVE SHOCKING PINK WITHOUT SCHIAPARELLI?

Elsa Schiaparelli was the high priestess of color, the queen of trompe l'oeil. Her famous friendships with artists and writers inspired many creations— Dalí once painted a lobster on an evening dress, and illustrator Christian Bérard's hand-drawn Medusa on a cape was sewn with sequins.

COMBINATIONS

pink + ORANGE

pink + BROWN

pink + TURQUOISE

While driving a red convertible, Dorothy Malone's sultry character in *Written on the Wind* (1956) wears a bright coral sleeveless dress with a long deep pink scarf tied at her neck.

'Angel Cheeks', 'Avant Garde', 'Break of Day', 'Pillow Talk', 'Raspberry Sundae', and 'Vogue' are all pink herbaceous peonies grown in the United States.

Author Jacqueline Susann typed *Valley of the Dolls* on a hot pink IBM Selectric typewriter.

seeing pink in a dream indicates happy times to come · 35

YELLOW

"I think of yellow as an accent to be used sparingly but confidently.
Since a little bit of yellow goes a long way, I like when it's used as a surprise,
such as for the lining of a black-and-white clutch. Yellow piping and trim
also add the right pop with this tricky color."

Fantasy fish, based on a pâte de
verre brooch by Gripoix, c. 1960

As the color of confidence, yellow symbolizes
energy, wisdom, and joy. From its good
visibility—think taxicabs—to its overpowering
optimism, yellow is an attention-getter.

HOW ABOUT...

A wide-brimmed yellow straw
hat to shield a freckle-prone
nose from the sun.

A buttery-colored cashmere
scarf tied snugly at the neck
of a charcoal peacoat.

Golden dahlias printed on a
circle skirt, worn with a navy
cable sweater on a cold and
snowy day.

ENDURING STYLE...
THE POST-IT NOTE (1979)

This relative newcomer to the canon of fine design never needed
to muscle its way into the pantheon: its handiness and its reusable
adhesive made it an instant shoo-in. The original pale yellow
Post-its have since been added to; you can now get them in nearly
every color imaginable (except black, perhaps) and in stripes, too.

As First Lady, Jacqueline Kennedy Onassis wore this dress from Chez Ninon to a White House dinner with the president of Peru.

COMBINATIONS

yellow + **GREEN**

yellow + **NAVY** + **PINK**

yellow + **BLACK** + **WHITE**

In *Dick Tracy*, Warren Beatty as the title character wears a sumptuous, deep yellow trench coat, a sure sign of his magnetism and importance.

"ANDY'S PARTIAL TO THE EASY CHEERFULNESS OF BLACK-EYED SUSANS."

Roger Vivier designed the pilgrim pump shoe for Yves Saint Laurent in 1965.

There are fewer than a dozen known yellow diamonds worldwide that are over 100 carats.

ORANGE

"Orange is one of those colors that seems so twentieth century, so happily modern. I never wear *just* orange, but I do love seeing it with other colors. It's amazing how this strong color can be chameleon-like when it's alongside a deep pink or navy."

Orange, the color of ambition, creativity, and fascination, is the happy compromise of aggressive red and cheerful yellow. This hot color rouses a sensation of heat, and is often associated with desire.

HOW ABOUT...

A little boy's striped T-shirt paired with Helmut Lang trousers and white Converse low-tops.

Opaque tangerine tights, a heather gray minidress, and short black patent leather boots for a showing of *A Clockwork Orange*.

A persimmon maillot under a sarong covered with swirling orange, red, and pink hibiscus.

YOU'RE NEVER TOO OLD TO TRICK OR TREAT.

"Andy found a bunch of these bags in a dime store, and as a playful gesture to Duchamp's readymades, he had labels sewn in them. We then used them one year in the office for Halloween."

Lounge by a pool in a
Moroccan caftan
and coral twig earrings.

Orange featured in the
Pop palette of the
1960s, as did anything
made by Courrèges.

COMBINATIONS

orange + **PINK**

persimmon + **NAVY**

orange + **WHITE**

The setting is autumn
suburbia, where Julianne
Moore as Cathy Whitaker in
Far from Heaven chats with
three women, all of whom
are dressed in a palette of
orange, from tangerine to
persimmon. Only Julianne
Moore's chiffon lavender
scarf adds contrast.

"TO DEFINE 'FEMININE' ONLY BY RUFFLES, A GIRDLE,
HIGH HEELS, AND SKIRTS THAT MUST BE PULLED DOWN ALL
THE TIME IS OBSOLETE, LIKE STEEL CORSETS AND GIRDLES."

— ANDRÉ COURRÈGES

BLUE

"In my wardrobe, turquoise blue is a staple, the way someone else might feel about navy blue. To me, turquoise pairs well with so many colors—with kelly green; with white; and with red and white it really pops. Turquoise blue with brown is pure luxury, especially if the blue is satin. Another special shade I've loved for years is French marine blue. Then again, one of my favorite sweaters is an old navy blue cable. I could never part with it."

Associated with status and dignity—think bluebloods, blue ribbons, and the bookish Bluestockings—this noble hue has influenced wardrobes throughout history. As for the blue of the sky, ancient Persians believed that the Earth rested upon an enormous sapphire, whose reflection colored the heavens above.

HOW ABOUT...

A navy-and-white striped sailor shirt worn with a bold rose print skirt.

A chunky turquoise necklace with your beau's crisp white shirt and black Capri pants —ideal for lunch on the Piazzetti Umberto.

A pair of blue seersucker pants and bare feet for the ferry ride to Shelter Island on a hot summer night.

THE CLASSIC SAINT-JAMES STRIPED NAUTICAL SHIRT IS NAVY AND RED, OR NAVY AND WHITE.

For Balenciaga, blues ranged from the clear iciness of aquamarine to the more exotic peacock blue. His chemise dress of the 1950s prefigured the no-care sheath a decade later.

COMBINATIONS

turquoise + **TANGERINE**

navy + **WATERMELON**

sky blue + **TAUPE**

Gwyneth Paltrow's character, Madge, in *The Talented Mr. Ripley* dons the perfect taupe raincoat over an elegantly cut sky-blue outfit.

Andy Warhol photographed the image of jeans on the Rolling Stones album cover *Sticky Fingers* (1971).

Dance your way into summer with blue ballet flats.

RED

"Red is one of those unafraid colors whose strength I admire. The shades I favor suggest depth and body. For instance, red lipstick can be the element that adds perfect color and contour to your face. On the other hand, when it gets too heavy then I feel it's too 'look at me,' which I'd never want to happen."

No color invokes the enigma of love like red. Its amorous connotations go back to Venus, the goddess of love, whose tears gave the red rose its color. When it comes to style, red signals passion: a lady in red is sure to be dynamic, strong-willed, and fiercely attractive.

HOW ABOUT...

A fire-engine-red cotton sundress and black heels for dinner in the garden at Raoul's.

Walking through the Tuileries in geranium-and-white striped mules.

Scarlet red mittens for making perfectly round snowballs.

Patsy Cline, Sophia Loren, and Madonna have all been known to wear a signature ruby-red lipstick.

COMBINATIONS

red + **CANARY YELLOW**

red + **NAVY**

coral + **PINK**

In Pedro Almodovar's *All About My Mother*, Sister Rosa, played by Penelope Cruz, wears a vibrant red coat with a pink headscarf.

"SOUP, BEAUTIFUL SOUP!"

First there was the humble soup itself, then Warhol's paintings of Campbell's Soup in the 1960s upended traditional ideas about the still life. The artist's wide-necked "souper dress" using the familiar red-and-white soup label also played off traditional American red-and-white gingham check.

For her coronation wardrobe, Queen Elizabeth II bought all the crimson silk available in London.

The Mercedes was named after Mercedes Jellinek, the daughter of the first person to buy this streamlined beauty.

BROWN

"Here's a color that cries out for companionship. I love to see it with pink and burnt orange, or else with cornflower blue, which is so elegant."

Often perceived as a masculine color, brown is indeed evocative of our fathers and grandfathers (mahogany desks, leather shave kits), but no one pulls off brown like a woman in winter. From tweed, herringbone, and gabardine to corduroy and camel hair, cozy textures in hues of brown are as practical and classic as the girls who wear them.

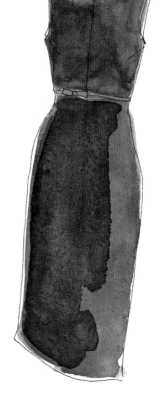

COMBINATIONS

mocha + **PINK**

taupe + chocolate brown

+ **CORNFLOWER**

brown + **BLACK** + **WHITE**

At a poolside cocktail party, one of Burt Lancaster's conquests in *The Swimmer* appears in a chocolate-brown V-neck sweater and a commanding brown-and-white harlequin hostess gown.

The L.L. Bean rubber boot—indispensable for outdoorsmen and urban preppies.

BEFORE YOU WERE A GIRL SCOUT, PERHAPS YOU WERE A BROWNIE...

For most little girls of a certain generation, their first brown dress was their Brownie uniform, with its bright orange necktie. Although Brownies were a junior division of the Girl Scouts, the name and theme derives from a book called *Brownies and Other Tales*, by Juliana Horatia Ewing (1886).

"I LOVE SEEING A DEEP BROWN WITH CANARY YELLOW."

Instead of black, choose chocolate brown for gloves that go up to your elbows.

HOW ABOUT...

Slipping on a mocha silk charmeuse sheath dress for the ballet. Add some sparkle with Kenneth Jay Lane's pink, amber, and multi-stone cocktail ring. Call it a night.

Tweed, tweed, tweed. Look smart in an espresso tweed blazer flecked with coral and raspberry and cinched at the waist with a leather bridal belt.

A set of deep chocolate leather luggage with amethyst crocodile trim. Travel to an exotic locale.

WHATEVER IT TAKES...

In 1977, a University of Pittsburgh art history professor made a pyramid of 45,600 Hostess Cupcakes as a visual ode to Dadaism and Pop Art. It was his way of connecting different eras in art, such as the pyramids of ancient Egypt and Warhol's soup cans.

BLACK

"I think women in black communicate greater sophistication than men in black—with the exception of Johnny Cash, who looked great in black. In New York, it's easy to overdo wearing black, because in the end I feel black is most potent when reserved for dressing up."

"WITH A BLACK PULLOVER AND TEN ROWS OF PEARLS, CHANEL REVOLUTIONIZED FASHION."

—CHRISTIAN DIOR

Black is said to be the absence of color altogether, hence its many meanings of emptiness, loss, anarchy, and mourning. Despite its history of negative connotations, no one can dispute the seductive, mysterious qualities and unrivaled elegance of what Renoir considered the "queen of colors."

HOW ABOUT...

Heading downtown with a zebra print bag holding the evening's necessities— Cherries in the Snow red lipstick, keys, and a $100 bill.

A Martin Grant raincoat in black poplin. Fasten a bug pin on the lapel. Wear it over black cigarette pants and don't worry about what you're wearing underneath —keep your coat on all day.

Wrist-short ink-black gloves trimmed with ostrich feathers for an evening at the opera.

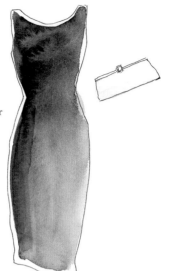

"It would be chic to wear a black wool dress inset with a white band of leather and to carry a white clutch. I might even accent it with a predominantly black-and-white tweed jacket."

ENDURING STYLE...
THE LITTLE BLACK DRESS

Thanks to Coco Chanel, the black dress became a fashion statement in 1919. Jump ahead to the 1950s (after Prohibition and before anyone had an inkling of what was in store for them in the late 1960s), when cocktail parties were in vogue and so was the little black dress—this time considerably shorter and more feminine. Even now, in the twenty-first century, the all-black dress remains a favorite of the au courant.

COMBINATIONS

black + **WHITE**

black + **GREEN**

black + **TURQUOISE**

In the star-studded 1963 romp *The V.I.P.s,* Elsa Martinelli's character strides into Heathrow Airport wearing the quintessential black cape. She swirls around to reveal its bold black-and-white striped lining.

FILM NOIR—
THEN AND ALWAYS

The Third Man, Lady in the Lake, Farewell My Lovely,
The Last Seduction, Double Indemnity,
Sexy Beast, Femme Fatale, L.A. Confidential,
Dial M for Murder, Twilight, Red Rock

WHITE

"Wear white with caution, and wear it interestingly. I always like white to break up the color. So my thinking is that with primary or secondary colors, white is used to clarify."

White is the color of purity, truce, virginity, and heaven. There are winter whites (snowflakes and eggnog), and whites of spring and summer (Easter lilies and white sand). Women in white—brides, debutantes, and nurses—connote innocence and virtue, but none so coyly as Marilyn Monroe.

Tennis champion René Lacoste was dubbed the "alligator" by the American press in 1927. A few years later, Lacoste and his partner put the little alligator on a cotton piqué shirt—in tennis white, of course.

COMBINATIONS

white + **BLACK**

white + **KELLY GREEN**

white + **GREEN** + **PINK** + **TURQUOISE**

Elegance in white on the screen: Elizabeth Taylor's strapless dress in *A Place in the Sun*, Audrey Hepburn's wedding gown in *Funny Face*, and Marilyn Monroe's unforgettable halter-style dress in *The Seven Year Itch*.

MUSICAL SHADES OF WHITE

The White Album, The Beatles; *White Christmas*, Bing Crosby; *Mystery White Boy*, Jeff Buckley; *White Ladder*, David Gray; *Black & White Night*, Roy Orbison; *White Light/White Heat*, Velvet Underground; anything by the White Stripes.

LITERARY SHADES OF WHITE

The Woman in White
by Wilkie Collins

White Oleander
by Janet Fitch

Snow White and the Seven Dwarfs
by the brothers Grimm

White Teeth
by Zadie Smith

The White Hotel
by D. M. Thomas

The White Album
by Joan Didion

Essays of E. B. White
by E. B. White

HOW ABOUT...

Bold white sunglasses and a green-and-white striped scarf, neatly folded and tied snugly on the front of your forehead, for an afternoon at the U.S. Tennis Open.

A crisp look for the hostess in summer—a white linen shell and one long strand of pearls, tied in a loose knot, worn over French marine blue capris. Go barefoot.

Wearing all white just because it's sunny.

Striped T-shirts, heavy fisherman sweaters, and tiny tanks all look perfect with a perfectly white pair of Levi's.

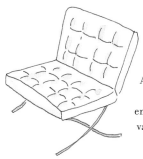

ENDURING STYLE...
THE BARCELONA CHAIR (1929)

Here's a chair that was first designed for royalty (Spain's King Alfonso XIII and his queen at the 1929 International Exposition in Barcelona) and has subsequently become an enduring emblem of great modernist design. When architect Ludwig Mies van der Rohe made the chair, it was with white leather and steel supports, a sly combination of luxury meets function.

PATTERN CRAZY

"Above all, I like to combine patterns—something striped with something floral, for example. I have always been partial to tweeds, which I think look great when paired with bright colors. It's the unexpected result that interests me."

Pattern, like everything else that speaks style, is deliberate. The width and repeat of a stripe is a measure that either *works*, or fails to inspire. Look in the grocery store: with a name like "wonder" and all those colorful polka dots, what child doesn't want to hug that happy-looking bag of soft bread?

"Lilly Pulitzer has always inspired me to take a strong position on color—everything about her clothes says 'Palm Beach,' especially her recurring motifs, such as the seahorses and shells. Then there is someone very modern like Paul Smith, who uses great prints. There's a lot of energy and humor in his clothes, but they are never, ever silly."

POLKA DOTS...

Dot candy—on paper rolls

Ladybugs (0 to 20 dots)

Dalmatians

Dice (no fewer than 1, no more than 12 dots)

Dotted swiss

Spectator shoes

Leopard ("never changes his spots")

Dominoes

Wonder Bread packaging (201 dots, small-size loaf)

NOT FOR SPECTATORS ONLY

Black and tan, black and white, or brown and white: these are the classic colors of the still-in-style spectator shoe. At its most basic, this two-tone oxford has black or brown leather at the toe cap and back, often with broguing—those nice little perforated dots that give the shoe its pop.

HUNGRY FOR STRIPES

"I came home one night, some months ago, and I went to the closet in my bedroom and a moth ate my sports jacket. He was laying on the floor, nauseous. It's a yellow and green striped jacket, you know. A little fat moth laying there, groaning. Part of the sleeve hanging out of his mouth. I gave him two plain brown socks. I said, 'Eat one now and eat one in a half-hour.'"

—Woody Allen, *Monologue*

STRIPES IN THE WORLD . . .

The American flag

Zebras

Rugby shirts

Barber shop poles

Candy canes

Hockney stripes

Breton sweaters

Poor boy shirts

Crosswalk

Black-and-white striped *anything*

Bumblebees

STRIPES IN THE CLOSET . . .

Bayadère, blazer, chalk, corduroy, gypsy, horizontal, nautical, pencil, pinstripe, regimental, roman, satin, seersucker, shadow, ticking, vertical.

A barrel chair and Louis XVI—both upholstered in patterns redolent of the timeless style of David Hicks.

A Missoni striped sweater, or as the Italians say, *un golf a righe di Missoni*

ACHIEVING YOUR STYLE AND LETTING GO OF STYLE

"Even when I was in my teens, I wasn't into fads. In fact, I've pretty much looked and dressed the same way for years, from my hair to my shoes (except the years 1974 to 1977, when I had the most embarrassing haircut). Maybe growing up in a house with five girls had something to do with it—carving out your individuality was a big deal. I do look to the past, but old-fashioned is just old. I want modernity without coldness. Femininity without fussiness. At least this is what works for me. And then there is my cardinal rule of shopping: Buy what you like."

BEING YOUR OWN STYLE GURU...

Let your closet be your guide. What do you tend to have? What do you love? Aspire to what makes you happy.

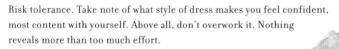

Look in the mirror. Height, size, and coloring all matter. Emphasize the positive. (Thin ankles? Wear capris.)

Risk tolerance. Take note of what style of dress makes you feel confident, most content with yourself. Above all, don't overwork it. Nothing reveals more than too much effort.

Basics are best. A smart pair of shoes or a well-cut coat (even a pair of jeans) always look good and last for years. "Investing in trends" is an oxymoron. Consider the Big Picture.

The Day-to-Day You. Dress yourself in clothes that work with how you spend your day. Make your clothes earn their keep—clothes that never leave the closet are freeloaders.

A size 6 is not a 6 is not a 6. Keep in mind which designers' clothing best suits your body—then stay the course.

Be stylish and multiply. If you love a certain pair of shoes or T-shirt, get more than one, and in other colors.

Put the cherry on the sundae. Don't be afraid to indulge yourself—be adventurous.

"IF YOU CAN CONVINCE YOURSELF YOU LOOK FABULOUS, THEN YOU CAN SAVE YOURSELF THE TROUBLE OF PRIMPING."

—ANDY WARHOL

"PETER PAN COLLAR > A BUSTIER"

"My advice is pretty simple: Think on your feet and
be resourceful. I don't fixate on a particular style.
I buy an object for no other reason than that I like it."

STYLE AS GESTURE,
STYLE AS PERSONAL SIGNATURE

Babe Paley tied her scarf on her handbag as she was
going to La Grenouille for lunch, and within a short time
a new fashion look came into being. Katharine Hepburn
always turned up her collars, both onscreen and in her
private life. (So has Diane Keaton.) Penelope Tree wore
the most mini of miniskirts. Björk likes swans. Fran
Lebowitz has a closet filled with button-down shirts.

"Things can be IN and OUT at the same time,
according to who does them."

—Robert Benton and Harvey Schmidt,
The In and Out Book

Whether you have a small empire of white T-shirts or you're pattern-crazy, one key to real
style—your *own* style—is becoming aware of what makes you feel most yourself out in the
world. You probably won't discover style in a magazine and you probably won't find it by
dressing like your best friend (who might not be flattered by being "imitated"). But the sure
path to your own style is trusting your instincts. Emphasize your inclinations. Strut *your* stuff.

"THE MOST
IMPORTANT THING
ABOUT BEAUTY
IS TO LEAVE
SOMETHING TO
THE IMAGINATION."

For the great Vionnet, whose draping and use
of cutting on the bias remain the standard in
haute couture, the woman and the garment
spoke in one voice: "When a woman smiles
the dress must smile with her."

"STYLE HAS TO BE EXACTLY IMPERFECT."

—ANDY SPADE

My hem is falling down
My stocking has a rip
My bra strap's sticking out
My zipper will not zip.

I'm wearing stripes with polka dots
Or giant floral prints
I'm in scarlet Marimekko
Or wall-to-wall in chintz.
Can this be me in culottes?
In a native Russian schmatte?
Did I really buy a poncho
So I look like a frittata?

—Nora Ephron, from "My Nightmare"

POSTURE

Style begins with stance, and how you look is first
conveyed by how you walk, or stand, or sit. Do you walk
confidently? Slumped over? Remember, style is not about
whether you're short, or very tall. Neither you nor your
clothes will appear stylish unless you stand straight and
greet the world with a sure and smart demeanor.

PERFECT POSTURE

Stand in front of a full-length mirror.

Rotate your knees slightly outward, and stand with your feet about a shoulder
width apart.

Pull in your stomach and tuck under your rear.

Release your shoulders and straighten your back. This will pull up your chest.

Align your head with your back and raise your chin parallel to the floor.

B—R—E—A—T—H—E

SECTION TWO

Style, Start to Finish

Everyday Style · In the Office
At Play · For a Party · Accessory Style
Seasonal Style · Travel Style

EVERYDAY STYLE

"Most days I'm in a skirt, heels, and my hair is pulled back. I love fun jewelry, so either I wear big earrings and lots of bracelets, or a pair of small earrings with a largish necklace. My idea of 'not dressing' is wearing a coat—the whole day. I adore coats, especially the kind you can wear indoors or out. If I'm in a hurry, I grab my favorite little trench coat, and I put it on over a simple skirt and sweater. I wrap myself up in it and wear it all day."

M T W T F S S

The alarm rings, the dog barks, and your closet beckons. This occurs with startling regularity. Like washing your face, seven-day style should be a natural reflex, attainable and satisfying.

FIT

A collar or jacket should lie comfortably at the back of your neck.

A long sleeve should fall just past the wrist bone when your arm is hanging at your side.

For bracelet sleeves, a jacket should stop one full inch above your wrist bone.

Your heel should not hang over the back of any shoe—whether it's a mule, slingback, or flip-flops.

To measure hips and bust, circle around the widest point.

Shoulder seams should sit properly at the crest of the shoulder.

A skirt hem should be straight, and parallel to the floor all around.

FORM

"Reduced to its simplest form, the feminine figure is either an I or an O or any one of the infinite number of intermediate stages. There are very few fashion problems for the I's, but plenty of them for the O's."

—Geneviève Antoine Dariaux

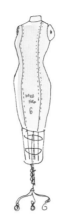

CLOSING THE GAP IN THE 20TH CENTURY...

1920s—slip on, over the head

1930s—side snaps

1940s—metal side zipper

1950s—back or side metal zipper

1960s—nylon zipper

1970s to present—nylon zipper uniformly used

KEEP IN MIND...

Fitted, but not too tight! (If you have to wiggle into something, assume it won't flatter you or your figure.)

Artificial cleavage is generally best avoided.

When purchasing new clothes or having them altered, try them on with the appropriate undergarments to make sure no unsightly panty lines or wrinkles will show.

SIZE CHART

	X-SMALL 0 2		SMALL 4 6		MEDIUM 8 10		LARGE 12 14	
BUST	32"	32½"	33½"	34½"	35½"	36½"	38"	39½"
WAIST	24"	24½"	25½"	26½"	27½"	28½"	30½"	31½"
HIP	34½"	35"	36"	37"	38"	39"	40½"	42"
BELT	24–28"		28–30"		30–32"		32–36"	

IN THE OFFICE

"To be honest, I don't dress that much differently in the office than when I'm not working. Sometimes my choice of colors or clothing is based on the weather or the meetings I have scheduled (or if I'm playing hooky and going to museums)."

Dressing for work means dressing for your company and your responsibilities. If your company has a dress code, apply your style within those parameters. If you see a lot of clients or customers, consider that what they see is also how they'll feel about you. Remember: no one ever gets reprimanded for dressing *well*.

Office furniture has style too, especially a Knoll chair.

CASUAL FRIDAY

"I know I should like 'casual Friday,' but in truth I find it silly. It's not that I feel there is only one right way to dress for work, and of course I want everyone who comes to our office to feel happy. Yet when staff show up in shorts and sneakers, it's as if they're saying good-bye before even saying good morning."

"WHEN I AM FLYING MY LITTLE PLANE, I USUALLY WEAR A SPORTS COSTUME WITH A RATHER FULL SKIRT AND A CLOSE-FITTING HAT."

—AMELIA EARHART

STYLE + WORK = POISE

Consider the type of job you have: whether you work in a corporate environment, at a fashion magazine, or in real estate, the sensibility of your job and your position will guide your dress choices.

Geography counts. Small town, big city, rural, or urban are relevant indicators of dress.

Draw attention to your work, not your dress. How you dress may be one way of communicating, but your performance is always the best way to "talk about" yourself to your colleagues or your boss.

Err on the side of discretion, not obsession: you might be proud of your tattoos and many earrings, but at work cover body markings and keep the earring count down to a pair—an earring on each earlobe.

Work style is not about a gym-fit figure but about demeanor: no matter how flat your stomach is, don't show it.

Blue hair, purple hair, overly hennaed hair, or architecturally spiked hair is best left to after-work hours.

Be observant. Some rules are spoken. Many others are unspoken.

For presentations or lectures, select something with color so that you won't fade into the background. Avoid looking washed-out.

"MY PHILOSOPHY IS TO LOOK PROFESSIONAL AND APPROACHABLE."

What's good for the goose is not good for the gander. Just because your boss might deviate from the normal office attire, don't copy her or him. (Or at least not until you're the boss and get to set the rules!)

Above all, be confident: posture and demeanor go a long way in an office. What you wear is part of the secure image you project.

AT PLAY

"When Andy and I met, I quickly realized he loved sports—he was always on his bike, or surfing, or trying out some new skateboard. I'm pretty much the opposite. But back then I would pretend that I loved nothing more than a hearty fifteen-mile bicycle ride. Thankfully, we've put that myth to rest."

TO THE BEACH

Forget rules. Banish the word *should* from your vocabulary. Play style is the best form of hedonism, and nothing says "free time" more than going to the beach. Sarongs are a must, and so is a little reading material. Besides that, what else is there but just you and the ocean?

ENDURING STYLE...
THE BIKINI (1946)

Arguably more incendiary than Dior's New Look (and preceding it by a year) was the bikini, designed by a Frenchman and shown at the Molitor Pool in Paris. The bikini (named after the Bikini atoll in the Pacific) was the first time fashion declared the navel a center of attention. Another decade would pass before the bikini was immortalized by Brigitte Bardot in the film *And God Created Woman*.

A DAY AT THE BEACH...

Sarong

Flip-flops

Water

Thermos of iced tea

Fruit, chips, and napkins

Oversize sweater and khakis
(for drinks at sunset)

Beach umbrella

Beach chair

Portable CD player

Magazines and a book

Kadima (perfect for a little exercise)

Disposable camera

Kites

A bag, of course!

Sunglasses

Big hat

Suntan lotion, lip balm
(protect, protect, protect)

WHO HAS THE BIGGER WAVE?
YOUR HAIR OR THE OCEAN?

In 1960, Americans put Brian Hyland's "Itsy Bitsy Teenie Weenie Yellow Polka Dot Bikini" at the top of the record charts.

In *To Catch a Thief*, when Cary Grant meets Grace Kelly in her hotel lobby on their way to a swim, she's all shoulders in a sleeveless black top and a swirl of white in an exaggerated A-line skirt. Her wide-brimmed white hat is in perfect proportion to her skirt. She's an architectural beauty.

IN THE NEIGHBORHOOD

Knock yourself out—go for a ride, cut some flowers. Just remember, no one has ever gotten a blister while snoozing in a hammock.

MUSIC FOR
THE BACKYARD...

Mosquitos, Misquitos

The Hissing of Summer Lawns,
Joni Mitchell

Trailer Park, Beth Orton

Activities: Swimming,
bicycling, talking,
sunbathing, napping,
barbecuing, playing
tennis, shooting hoops
or pool, brushing the dog

"TAKE A SCHWINN-BUILT VACATION!"

(1940 advertisement)

The bicycle's journey to the neighborhoods and side streets of America made headlines when Arnold, Schwinn & Company debuted the 1934 Streamline Aerocycle at the 1933 Centennial of Progress Exposition in Chicago. With its modernist design (So much chrome! So much color! Such a sturdy frame!) and low cost, the Aerocycle pedaled its way into the American heartland. Now kids, too, could take to the road. Every Schwinn bike, then as now, was "guaranteed for life."

"THE BICYCLE HAS DONE MORE FOR THE EMANCIPATION OF WOMEN THAN ANYTHING ELSE IN THE WORLD."
—SUSAN B. ANTHONY, 1896

To keep your hair off your face, how about tucking it under a big straw hat; wearing a bandana headband style; or pulling it back into a loose ponytail, held with a piece of striped grosgrain.

AT THE CABIN

You don't have to love hiking to spend a weekend at a cabin in the mountains. Enjoy the air. Have a country breakfast. Count the stars at night.

ENDURING STYLE...
NAVY PEACOAT (1886)

With its military-style symmetry, coarse wool, and telltale buttons, the peacoat first did battle protecting enlisted men against foul weather. Over time, the peacoat has become both a fashion classic as well as a symbol of sixties counterculture figures such as Allen Ginsberg and Bob Dylan.

MUSIC FOR
THE MOUNTAINS...

Circles, The Autumn Defense

Roses in the Snow, Emmylou Harris

Good Will Hunting, motion picture soundtrack

ENDURING STYLE...
L.L. BEAN TOTE BAG (1944)

Sixty years ago the L.L. Bean tote bag was made to carry ice. By the 1960s, contrasting trim was added and voilà—an icon of good design and style emerged. Its American-style familiarity makes this modest bag a companionable tote, good for holding everything from ice skates and mittens to gift wrap and scads of colorful ribbon.

Activities: Skiing, bird watching, building a fire, tobogganing, kayaking, picnicking, collecting leaves, breathing in the air

The traditional Fair Isle sweater, made in the Shetland Islands of Scotland, dates back more than 500 years.

FOR A PARTY

"Getting dressed for a party is the perfect way to get in the mood for the festivities. I do some planning in advance, but I always leave room for spontaneity. Or maybe this is a kinder way of saying that it's not always easy to decide on an outfit, which to me means my dress, coat, shoes, handbag (always small), and jewelry. One thing I never take with me to a party: business cards."

PARTY TOAST...

"Here's to sugar on the strawberries!"

—Burt Lancaster, from *The Swimmer*

INDULGE, INDULGE, INDULGE

Enjoy yourself. Become a walking dream. If you're lean on top, wear something with spaghetti straps. Got great legs?—Wear something with a slit. No cleavage? No problem—choose a deep V in back. Put your hair up, or shake it loose. Anything you should remember to ask yourself? Just this: can you walk in your shoes, sit down in your dress, lean over in front?

PARTY MUSIC...

Youth & Young Manhood, Kings of Leon

Electric Version, The New Pornographers

Velvet Underground & Nico, Velvet Underground (for the after-party)

"I love sparkly jewelry. If I want a little glitter around my face, I'll put some rhinestone clips in my hair. I have a collection of antique barrettes that Andy's given to me over the years."

WHAT IS ELEGANCE?

"Elegance is good taste
plus a dash of daring."

—Carmel Snow

PARTIES IN
THE MOVIES

Breakfast at Tiffany's

La Dolce Vita

Sabrina

The Party

Monsoon Wedding

Shampoo

ODE TO THE DRESS

"A dress can be the expression
of a state of mind. There
are dresses that sing of joy of life,
dresses that weep, dresses that
threaten. There are gay dresses,
mysterious dresses, pleasing
dresses, and tearful dresses."

—Paul Poiret

AS THE HOSTESS
OF THE PARTY...

The hostess gown had its heyday in the
1950s, yet nothing signals the confidence
and polish of a hostess more than a
sumptuous long-skirted ensemble.
The generous proportions of a hostess
gown (a variation is known as hostess or
palazzo pants) allow you to do all the
things a hostess must be prepared
for: fly into the kitchen, clean up a
spilled drink, move in and out of
conversations with your guests.

Needle, needle, dip and dart,
Thrusting up and down,
Where's the man could ease a heart
Like a satin gown?

—Dorothy Parker,
from "The Satin Dress"

ACCESSORY STYLE

"Without question, accessories are the favorite part of my wardrobe.
I could easily wear the same little top and pants every day as long
as I could change my jewelry or my handbags at whim. I think your
personality is uniquely expressed through your choice of accessories.
It's the easiest form of self-declaration."

An arsenal of accessories will prepare you with
ammunition for any condition, circumstance, or climate.
Wearing all black? Put on pink sandals with little
rhinestones. Need a lift? Wear high heels. Want to hide?
Wear a hat. More than any element in a woman's
wardrobe, accessories allow for easy creativity. But with
all this possible pleasure at your fingertips, remember
that balance and restraint are important ingredients, too.

Gloves with a trim
of confetti-like fur
are a feminine
understatement.

The majordomo of 1960s
costume jewelry is
Kenneth Jay Lane.

"OF COURSE I BELIEVE THAT LESS IS MORE,
BUT THE *LESS* HAS TO BE *MORE*."

With polished pink toenails in the summer
or patterned tights in the winter, this
open-toe shoe always looks sophisticated.

HANDBAGS

"This is where style and utility are most ideally paired.
I started designing bags simply because I couldn't find one that
balanced these qualities perfectly."

"The first bag that I designed was actually
based on an antique STRAW bag. It was boxy,
perfectly square, and very, very simple. It
was open at the top, but because I carried
it year-round I would tie it closed with a
scarf in the winter to keep out the snow."

"My handbag designs have been influenced by the
great old traveling TRAIN CASES and hat boxes that always
had such nice little handles. Round or square train cases such as the
luggage made by Goyard appeal to me. One of my favorite movie scenes
is in *Rear Window* when Grace Kelly opens her Mark Cross case at
Jimmy Stewart's. It's a perfect moment of chic understatement."

SPEAKING OF HANDBAGS...

"There are a number of fabrics that I think are great for handbags:
Harris tweeds, especially those that are brightly colored, such
as a combination of raspberry, orange, green, and brown;
herringbone, in pink and bordeaux. Anything with straw or
wicker, satin, BOARSKIN LEATHER, and of course canvas."

HANDBAG PRIMER

BASKET—Open or closed. The body of the bag is made with woven wicker or straw.

BIRKIN—Already an Hermès classic, dating from 1984. Similar to the Kelly bag.

BOX—The handles may vary but the shape is the same: either a square or rectangle with four hard corners.

BUCKET—Its name comes from its former utilitarian use, making this round-bottomed, open-topped bag today an example of practicality.

DRAWSTRING—Like the bucket bag, but this one closes with the use of a drawstring.

HOBO—A large, soft bag, usually with a zipper and a shoulder strap, that sags or is slightly crushed when hung from the shoulder.

TOTE (also known as a "shopper")—The paper bag is the paradigm for this ubiquitous open-topped bag with straplike handles. Typically made of a sturdy material, such as cotton canvas or leather. Indispensable in cities like New York, where women walk more places than they drive.

WRISTLET—A small bag with a thin strap intended to dangle from the wrist.

CLUTCH—Forget handles. This bag, often used as an evening bag, is meant to be carried in the hand and has been a fashion fixture since the early twentieth century.

KELLY—Although the style dates back to 1892, it became popularly known as the Kelly bag in 1956, when Grace Kelly, posing for the cover of *Life* magazine, used it to cover her pregnancy.

THE NANTUCKET LIGHTSHIP BASKET

No other American bag is so identified with a place as the Nantucket purse, which dates back to 1856. The bags were so named because the wooden molds were made from the masts on the lightships. Nearly a hundred years later, in 1948, a woven lid was added and the popular handbag was launched—the ladies-who-yacht club were seen carrying these bags in posh ports from Nantucket Island to the French Riviera.

HANDBAG CARE

When it comes to your LEATHER BAGS, be sure to keep them dust-free and wipe them with a slightly damp cloth. If you use special cleaning products, keep in mind that a little is better than a lot. You can also use a damp cloth on PATENT LEATHER bags, along with a mild detergent, if needed. An art eraser is a handy way to remove slight marks and soil spots on PIGSKIN. Use a lint brush or roller to clean up FABRIC purses (especially worth doing if you have dogs or cats). Luxury coverings such as SATIN or bags with RHINESTONES are best cleaned by a quality dry cleaner.

STORE your handbags in a relatively cool place, away from heat and direct sunlight. Instead of using plastic bags or containers, opt for soft cloth pouches to keep the bags from becoming scuffed or dusty. Use little string tags to identify your bags.

"When I think about some of the handbags we've done, I'm still partial to the box shape we launched our company with. Its original name is the Medium Shopper. Today I think of it as our classic. I also love a bag we call Quinn."

"I love envelope bags — the really flat ones are ideal. Sometimes I use our photo envelope as a bag and I'm able to fit in everything I need."

THE CASHIN CARRY

A handbag by Bonnie Cashin exuded bright colors and modernity, with features like industrial toggles as closures. Coin purses were applied to the outside of the bag ("the Cashin Carry"), and the bag itself was sometimes actually stitched onto a coat or dress. Cashin, who made purses for on-the-go women like herself, was known to wear three bags on one arm when the need arose.

Louis Vuitton's bucket-shaped Noe bag of 1932 was originally designed to carry five bottles of champagne.

"A pouch with a drawstring over your wrist is great at a cocktail party."

SHOES

"I love slingbacks, all year round. Because I like a certain lightness to a shoe, I've never been fond of heavy shoes. Slingbacks make it possible to stay light, even when the toe of a shoe is more pronounced, such as when it's super-rounded, or very pointed. I also think the cut of a shoe makes all the difference. If a design makes the foot look pretty, then the shoe is talking to me."

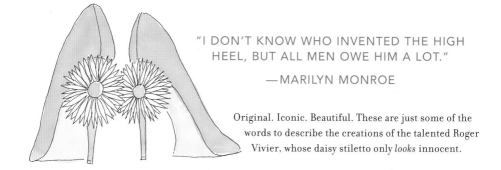

"I DON'T KNOW WHO INVENTED THE HIGH HEEL, BUT ALL MEN OWE HIM A LOT."

—MARILYN MONROE

Original. Iconic. Beautiful. These are just some of the words to describe the creations of the talented Roger Vivier, whose daisy stiletto only *looks* innocent.

JUST A LITTLE BOW...

Once known as "the Foxcroft sneaker" for its frequent appearance on schoolgirls at the Foxcroft School, the Belgian loafer remains the model for a perfect moccasin shoe. Henri Bendel first spotted the Belgian loafer when he was in Belgium in the late 1940s, where they were used as country slippers. The hard sole and hand-sewn craftsmanship appealed to Bendel, who began marketing them in New York at a little midtown shop by the mid-1950s. The first Belgian loafer sold for $12.50. Today, they cost considerably more, and like their predecessors, are entirely hand-sewn, right down to the signature leather bow and contrast piping.

"When a shoe is pretty or elegant it communicates to me that the woman is pretty sexy."

—Andy Spade

"SHOES SHOULD BE 'LIGHT AND FLEET.'"
—VALENTINA

Who needs a flashlight?
These rhinestone and
peau de soie sandals
are sparkle aplenty for
partying outdoors.

MORE SHOES, MORE STYLES...

Flip-flops, espadrilles (made famous by the fashionable on the Riviera in the early 1900s), bucks, moccasins, Converse All Stars, go-go boots, saddle shoes, Hush Puppies, Wellingtons, riding boots, slippers.

The heat index shoots up when you combine nighttime black with hot pink.

They looked good on Harlow and they'll look good on you—just blow on the puff of this little marabou slipper.

STILL IN STYLE: SHOES FROM OUR CHILDHOOD

BROGUES—The neatly pinked brown leather tongue and perforated brogue moved into the style echelon in the 1930s, when the Prince of Wales deemed this peasant shoe fitting for a round of golf. Since then, the brogue has become a classic golf shoe.

PENNY LOAFERS—It began life as a Bass Weejun but earned its nickname "penny loafer" in the 1950s when putting a penny in the little leather slot became trendy. In New York City, some people substituted a subway token for a penny.

The Mary Jane shoe got its name from a character in the Buster Brown comic strip in 1902.

JEWELRY

"Gold with color is pretty and makes everything you're wearing shine a bit more. I tend to layer my bracelets, whereas I go for one big necklace rather than combining several. And I don't wear a lot of rings, but I do have a weakness for big old cocktail rings."

ENDURING STYLE...
CARTIER TRINITY RING (1924)

Peerless for its simplicity and skillful execution, the tri-gold ring symbolizes love, fidelity, and friendship in its use of pink, yellow, and white gold respectively. Jeweler Louis Cartier designed the ring for his friend, the poet Jean Cocteau.

A sumptuous coral, emerald, and diamond Cartier choker owned by the Duchess of Windsor.

Babe Paley wore her pearls wrapped multiple times around her wrist, along with other colorful stone and gold bracelets.

THE COCKTAIL RING...

Large is the best way to characterize the cocktail ring, which came into vogue in the 1950s. Typically, a cocktail ring is set with varied stones in some sort of pattern and tends to have a high dome, making it less than ideal for wearing under gloves but perfect when holding a glass of champagne.

COSTUME JEWELRY

Rhinestones, colored stones, simulated pearls, enamel . . .
all are elements found in costume jewelry. While it seems
hardy, costume jewelry actually is less forgiving of time and
wear than fine jewelry: the luster chips, settings loosen,
adhesives dry out. The first rule of costume jewelry is to wear it
and enjoy it. The second rule: a bit of care will go a long way.

WRIST APPEAL

Wear cuff bracelets on both wrists. Diana
Vreeland was known for the Verdura cuffs she
wore, and American sportswear designer Claire
McCardell designed her matching tooled
leather cuffs. Or combine your gold and sparkly
bracelets and wear all of them on one wrist.
Keep the rest of your wardrobe simple.

A striped grosgrain
ribbon always
looks good with a
classic watch face.

ADORNMENTS . . .

Bangles

Signet rings

Cocktail rings

Big earrings

Chunky necklaces

Turquoise

Kenneth Jay Lane "originals"

Charm bracelets

Ted Muehling
earrings

Vegetable necklace, designed
by Karl Lagerfeld, late 1980s

Vivien Leigh had a
cocktail ring with
twenty-five diamonds.

Coral necklaces,
bracelets, rings

SUNGLASSES

"Sunglasses have an amazing style quotient—there's something so strong and mysterious about them. Some glasses say 'Buzz off.' Others pull you in and make you want to know more about the person behind the sunglasses. Frankly, I always have at least two pairs in my purse."

SUNGLASS STYLES THAT MAKE ME SMILE...

Headband glasses, tortoiseshell, cat-eyes, Dr. Scholl's Health Glasses, wrap-around, tinted lenses, aviators, bubble wraps, pearl frames.

"Ann Slater is the most inspiring example of someone who wears glasses well. Hers don't say 'Go away.'"

THE RAY-BAN: A TRIUMPH OF FORM AND FUNCTION

When the Army Air Corps commissioned Bausch & Lomb to make them sunglasses in the 1930s, they had a few specifications for the manufacturer: the frames needed to curve below the eye because pilots were often looking down at an instrument panel, and the lenses would need to protect the pilots from the strong glare at high altitudes. Hence the Ray-Ban: an aviator's friend, making it safer for them to fly. By the 1960s, Ray-Bans were a fashion accessory, and have been so ever since.

YOU KNOW THEM BY THEIR GLASSES...

Andy Warhol

Ann Slater

Le Corbusier

John Lennon

Woody Allen

Pauline Trigère

Peter Sellers

Anna Wintour

Philip Johnson

Swifty Lazar

Jackie Onassis

Carrie Donovan

Edith Head

Elvis Costello

Londoner Oliver Goldsmith became one of the first "name" eyewear designers by having celebrities such as Lord Snowdon, Nancy Sinatra, and John Lennon wear his glasses.

GLASSES, HOLLYWOOD STYLE

Once Hollywood became enamored of sunglasses (recall the Foster Grant ads of the 1960s), they were de rigueur for celebrities. Diane Keaton in *Annie Hall* made granny glasses a hip accessory of the 1970s; Robert Redford in Vuarnets was the perfect ski stud in *Downhill Racer*; and Jack Nicholson has made the Wayfarer a trademark uniquely his, both on and off camera.

HATS

"I find that hats are just the thing for adding wit and personality.
I insist on wearing a hat whenever I'm in the sun, but I'm just as inclined
to wear a wide-brimmed hat indoors if my hair is 'misbehaving.'"

A HAT IS NICE TO WEAR 365 DAYS A YEAR

BERET—Soft, unstructured, and snug-fitting; made popular by the French.

BONNET—Hard or soft brimmed hat with a ribbon that ties under the chin.

CLOCHE—Close-fitting hat with a high crown and narrow brim.

COOLIE HAT—Triangular-shaped plush felt. Valentina described them
as resembling Chinese roofs.

FEZ—Brimless, with a high cylindrical crown and tassel.

GARDEN PARTY—Wide-brimmed, soft straw hat, often decorated with
ribbons and flowers.

ANDY'S
FAVORITE
SKI CAP

LAMPSHADE—Low crown with a wide, gently slanting brim. In the early 1960s, Christian Dior
made some exceptional hats using this silhouette.

NEHRU—Soft, brimless hat with a creased crown.

PICTURE—Large hat whose floppy brim frames the face.

PILLBOX—Small, round, brimless women's hat. Balenciaga was known for his "hard-edged" pillbox
hats. Halston's pillbox hat became fashionable when worn by then First Lady Jacqueline Kennedy.

PROFILE—The brim is turned up on one side and down on the other. Faye Dunaway wore one in
The Thomas Crown Affair.

SAILOR—Usually made of cotton canvas for durability, having a low crown and stiff brim.

SKI CAP—Knitted hat with a wide, upturned cuff, often finished with a pom-pom on top.

TAM O'SHANTER—Scottish hat whose round, flat top is adorned with a pom-pom.

TOQUE—Small, structured, and brimless.

TURBAN—Draped fabric that fits around the head. Popular in the 1920s, although renowned
fashion publicist Eleanor Lambert wore turbans for decades.

VISOR—A crownless hat with a rounded front brim. Schiaparelli was partial to clothing for sports,
and included a straw visor among her creations.

HAT CHART

HEAD SIZE (inches)	HAT SIZE	
21"	6⅝	S
21½"	6½	S
21⅝"	6⅞	S
22⅛"	7	M
22½"	7⅛	M
23"	7¼	L
23⅜"	7⅜	L
23½"	7½	XL
24"	7⅝	XL
24½"	7¾	XXL
25"	7⅞	XXL

"My favorite shape
in herringbone"

"A hat must be everything or nothing
. . . [either] so terribly chic and beautiful
that it forces you to its mood, or a little
something that is nothing—a cap, a hood
that covers your hair and makes you sleek."

—Valentina

Chanel, who began her
career as a milliner,
designed the boater
in 1910 for wearing at
the racecourse in the
French Midi.

Jacques Heim's
pleated seaside hat
from the 1940s is ideal
even for city creatures.

SEASONAL STYLE

"Of course some of my clothing choices are specific to a season—I practically live in cashmere cable jewel-neck sweaters during the cool months—but I also have a few quirks. For instance, no matter how cold it is, I never wear stockings. Yet I admire them on other women."

SPRING

"I know it sounds trite, but it's true . . . spring is a tonic for getting things done. Whether it means cutting my hair or moving around the furniture at home, the nicer weather makes me want to be active."

FLY ME TO THE MOON
LET ME PLAY AMONG THE STARS,
LET ME SEE WHAT SPRING IS LIKE
ON JUPITER AND MARS . . .

— "FLY ME TO THE MOON"

RAIN BOOTS

Spring is for shedding—those layers of winter clothing you've been carting around (knit caps, four-foot-long scarves) return to the closet for another year. Spring is a time for the mackintosh and the umbrella, and when you swap the fur boot for the rain boot. Gloves, if used at all, are more for show than need.

Spring can also be a little confusing: the mornings and those late afternoons in the shade are still cool, yet mid-day is wonderfully warm. So do you wear shorts with kneesocks? A brown leather jacket with deep orange Capris? Ride in the convertible with the windows up and the heat on?

SUMMER

"This is where Andy and I are completely different from one another. Andy's idea of summer is swimming in the ocean, running, or bicycling, pretty much anything that involves movement. My idea of the perfect summer activity is 'magazining'— a friend and I will first stock up on magazines and then come back to the house, where we settle in for an afternoon on the patio—out of the sun."

BERMUDA SHORTS

The name is a misnomer, since Bermuda shorts did not in fact originate in Bermuda. British military officers, serving in the tropics, cut off their pant legs at the knee, thus creating the knee-length shorts. Proper sartorial style with these madras or brightly colored shorts includes knee-length socks, but in America the socks stay in the drawer.

"I'm addicted to these Mexican embroidered tops, which over the years have become my standard wardrobe on the weekends."

Summer rain is the gentlest of all . . . perfect for capris, flip-flops, and a blue and white sailor's hat, such as this one designed by Virginia Johnson.

Flip-flops with a soft flower will make you smile. Splash on perfume with lots of floral notes.

FALL

"Indian summer is great, but after August in New York I can't wait for the return of cool nights. I much prefer a great scarf and jacket to a little cotton dress. Then again, there's always that moment when the seasons cross over one another. For example, in early fall I might wear a wool cable jewel-neck sweater with a cotton floral skirt and open-toed slingbacks. Sometimes it doesn't matter what the season is—I just wear what I like."

"I don't ride horses, but that doesn't stop me from enjoying a little riding jacket nipped in at the waist and taking Henry on a long walk."

"I love when the temperature drops below 50 degrees; that's when a pretty scarf is just the solution to cut the chill."

HOW TO SPOT A PERFECTLY MADE UMBRELLA...

Cane handles (tulipwood is used for the shaft in a two-piece handle)

Tempered steel frame to ensure flexibility and wind resistance

Ribs and stretchers are hand-wired together

A cover of fine quality nylon or waterproofed English silk

Mother-of-pearl button fastener

AUTUMN SHOWERS

Since the 1750s, the best umbrellas have been made in England by Brigg, maker of umbrellas for the royal family.

WINTER

"I'm a cold-weather person and think nothing of layering sweaters and wrapping a big scarf around my neck. Most of my friends prefer the indoors when it's cold outside, but I don't—this is a season I thrive in. Though I do confess snow can get pretty grimy and slushy in New York—and that's not fun."

People tend to shy away from strong colors in winter, but in fact this is when color is at its uninflected purest: reds are deeper, browns richer, even ivory is dreamier than ever. Orange on a gray day is a beacon of warmth; turquoise adds glamour and personality.

APRÈS-SKI (OR WHENEVER YOU'RE GOING TO SEE MORE SNOW THAN PEOPLE)...

Faux fur hat with flaps

Earmuffs

Bright orange ski parka

Pink ski pants (why not?)

Warm, furry slip-on boots (they can double as slippers)

Flannel pajamas

Sunglasses (beware of snow glare)

Protective face cream against windburn, lip balm

Thermos for hot chocolate

Mittens

Buying a great wool coat is "investment dressing."

Snow day! Time for your oldest Norwegian sweater, mukluks, and your flannel pajama bottoms. Make a fire and read *Ethan Frome*, by Edith Wharton.

TRAVEL STYLE

"Andy and I like to take a couple of long trips every year, but our calendar is also filled with shorter trips, for business or for being with friends and family. I've gotten better at deciding what to pack, but in my definition of essentials accessories far outweigh basics."

"TRAVEL STYLE ISN'T JUST ABOUT YOUR LUGGAGE. IT'S ABOUT HOW YOU GET FROM ONE PLACE TO ANOTHER."

MARK CROSS—AMERICAN DESTINY

Gerald Murphy, artist and bon vivant, inherited the Mark Cross company from his father in the 1930s. Murphy and his wife, Sara, were F. Scott Fitzgerald's models for the tragic figures of Dick and Nicole Diver in *Tender Is the Night*. With the Fitzgeralds, Hemingway, Picasso, and Dorothy Parker, among others, the Murphys made "living well is the best revenge" (Gerald coined the phrase) their storied existence in America and on the French Riviera.

TRAVEL BOOKS

I Married Adventure by Osa Johnson

2001: A Space Odyssey by Arthur C. Clarke

Between Meals: An Appetite for Paris by A. J. Liebling

The Alexandria Quartet by Lawrence Durrell

On the Road by Jack Kerouac

Two Towns in Provence by M.F.K. Fisher

When *Catcher in the Rye*'s Holden Caulfield goes off to boarding school, his assortment of urban status symbols includes Mark Cross leather luggage.

Scarves and gloves are versatile accessories and always easy to pack. Besides, a scarf always fits, no matter what size you are.

"Maybe they won't add to the beauty of the world or the life of men's souls—I'm not sure. But automobiles have come and almost all outward things are going to be different because of what they bring."

—Joseph Cotton, in *The Magnificent Ambersons*

PLACES WITH STYLE

Hyannis Port

The East Village

Nantucket

Newport

Palm Beach

Paris

Positano

Saint-Tropez

Savannah

76th and Madison Avenue

Silver Lake

Telluride

Venice

MUSIC FOR ROAD TRIPS

Highway 61 Revisited, Bob Dylan

Being There, Wilco

Nebraska, Bruce Springsteen

ENDURING STYLE...
VOLKSWAGEN BEETLE (1931)

Beetles, punch-bugs, beach buggies, the 1960s, cross-country trips, slower times. The German VW, with its hallmark curve, soon became an icon of a casual America, a happy pod on the road. Reintroduction in 1998 has proven its popularity as everybody's favorite car. Let the good times roll.

Raymond Loewy's 1953 Studebaker Starliner was the first American car to be exhibited at the Museum of Modern Art, New York.

"ISN'T IT WONDERFUL TO UNPACK WOOL JERSEY AND THUMB YOUR NOSE AT AN IRON?"

—CLAIRE MCCARDELL

TRAVEL TIPS

Take water—The best way to stay healthy and look healthy. Be sure to drink water before, during, and after a long trip.

Soft peds—If you get cold feet, these are almost as good as the comfy slippers you kept at home.

Cosmetic and beauty samples—Perfect for short trips.

Travel candle—"I always pack a few candles and put them all around my hotel room. It makes me feel more at home and less like I'm in an unfamiliar place."

Travel iron/steamer—Despite your best intentions, some clothes do wrinkle. Save on hotel laundering services by packing a lightweight steamer or iron.

THE HOTEL SCHMOTEL

"As much as I love a beautiful room when we go away, it has to be practical. I like a place that has been designed to *work*— where my cosmetic bags won't slip off a counter, for instance. If a hotel stay isn't effortless then it's not enjoyable."

"Sometimes the fun part in going to Boston is taking the train instead of the shuttle, because it *feels* like the right speed."

"LV"

Louis Vuitton was the exclusive packer for Empress Eugénie, the wife of Napoleon III, when he got the idea to make flat-topped trunks. He persuaded cruise ships to accommodate his new luggage, which soon became the leading choice for travel gear. Vuitton, who opened shop in Paris in 1854, was also commissioned by an Indian maharajah to make a travel case for his tea service that even included a silver container for carrying water.

WHAT SIZE CLOTHES DO YOU WEAR?

AMERICAN	BRITISH	CONTINENTAL	JAPANESE
2	8	34	5
4	10	36	7
6	12	38	9
8	14	40	11
10	16	42	13
12	18	44	15
14	20	46	17

WHAT SIZE SHOE DO YOU WEAR?

AMERICAN	BRITISH	CONTINENTAL	JAPANESE
6	3	35½	23
6½	3½	36	23½
7	4	37	24
7½	4½	37½	24½
8	5	38	25
8½	5½	38½	25½
9	6	39	26
9½	6½	40	26½
10	7	41	27

MEXICO

"Mexico has become like a second home to us. Each year we go for a long stay, and as soon as I step off the plane, I let out a big sigh of relief."

INSIDE MY SUITCASE FOR A TRIP TO MEXICO

Bright bikinis ("My favorites are little cotton bikinis I found in Positano. Some are polka dots, others are Provençal prints.")

Black-and-white cotton cigarette pants

Pink silk shantung Capri pants

Mexican dresses ("I purchased these during other trips over the years.")

Big straw hat ("I've never been one for lying in the sun.")

French blue-and-white striped T-shirt

Pink sandals decorated with a rhinestone dragonfly

Classic espadrilles

Stone capri sandals ("Inspired by a trip to Capri—where else?")

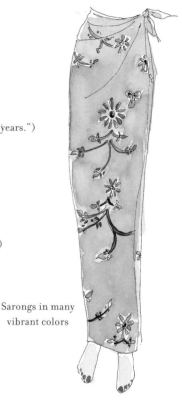

Sarongs in many vibrant colors

Cotton pajamas

CARRY-ON:

Bottled water

Magazines ("I never have enough time to read.")

Sunglasses in different colors

Jewelry (overscale earrings, tear-shaped drops, lots of bracelets)

Multicolored travel wallet

Portable CD player (with mini speakers and favorite CDs)

Hair and beauty products

Travel candles

KANSAS CITY

"In our office we have a few clocks showing the time in different cities. One of them is for Kansas City, where I grew up. I see that clock every day and it's a reminder not only of where I came from, but who I am."

INSIDE MY SUITCASE FOR A TRIP TO KANSAS CITY

Full skirts, in solids and prints ("My sisters still tease me about wearing skirts, but I love them.")

A wide red leather headband, some polka-dot scarves, and a few barrettes with brightly colored rhinestones for my hair

Slim-fitting pants

Square-toed flats

Kitten-heel slingbacks

Linen Chinese pajamas ("The ones with silk frog closures are so pretty.")

CARRY-ON:
Bottled water

A good book

Some work from the office ("but not too much")

Fitted sweaters, all of them jewel-neck pullovers

Jewelry ("I don't have a lot of jewelry, so I wear what I have over and over.")

Photo of Andy

"You can't take Kansas City out of the girl. Kate's background is actively in the fore-ground because it's part of her barometer."

—Andy Spade

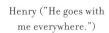

Henry ("He goes with me everywhere.")

WHO SAYS YOU CAN'T GO HOME AGAIN?

Maintaining Style

FOREVER CLOTHES

"No matter how much I might be captivated by a new floral skirt or another jewel-neck sweater, there are some things in my closet that I can't imagine *not* having around. It's like holding on to certain treasured books—they continue to 'speak' to you, so why give them away? Besides, as far as I'm concerned, you shouldn't be allowed to give away anything until you're forty-five."

"OLD CLOTHES ARE OLD FRIENDS."

—CHANEL

ENDURING STYLE...

Stadium blankets, white tennis balls, button-down shirts, *The Graduate*, hula hoops, martinis, Bermuda shorts, patio dinners, *Catcher in the Rye*, jazz, Hershey's Kisses, hammocks, Shetland sweaters, cold beer, the bikini, blue jeans, barbecues, navy blue Keds, the seesaw, the Zippo lighter, *Le Ballon Rouge*.

KATE'S FOREVER CLOTHES...

School uniform blazer—"I still wear it—it's navy with a white monogram."

Fisherman sweater—"My father brought this back from Ireland years ago. Even though it's kind of stretched-out, it's great for a cool day at the beach."

Double-drop pearl earrings—"These are very special and came from my grandmother."

Tiaras—"Actually, these belonged to my mother and I was thrilled when none of my sisters wanted them. I'm just now thinking about wearing them ..."

Raw coral bracelet—"It was my great-aunt's and even though the coral is a bit brittle, I can't part with it."

WARDROBE CLASSICS

"After a few years of building a wardrobe, I think you get to a point where it becomes obvious what sorts of things you gravitate toward. I have friends who wear polo shirts year-round, and other friends who don't even own one. Wardrobe classics are the fundamentals of your own style."

KATE'S WARDROBE CLASSICS...

Full skirts—"These definitely go at the top of my list."

Jewel-neck sweaters—"I love these sweaters. Mine are always long sleeve and in every possible color, flat and cable, wool or cashmere. But they're never cotton."

French-striped bateau tops—"I don't wear T-shirts, but I am addicted to these French classics."

Coats—"I prefer three-quarter-length coats that have a slim fit, and that are neither oversized nor with a raglan sleeve. I love to wear them with a sweater and pants."

Earrings made by Ted Muehling—"I'm hooked on these earrings. It's that simple."

Quartz pendant necklace—"A favorite I wear all the time. There's a tiny scarab on the setting."

A WORD ABOUT MONOGRAMS...

"I don't think you should wear a lot of monograms, but they do look great when centered on a jewel-neck sweater in classic script. Block lettering is fine, but I would only use it on a tote. Frankly, I prefer script lettering even on a tote. Some accessories cry out to be personalized with monograms, such as the lining of a really gorgeous bag, or the back of an old watch. And I always prefer a three-letter monogram. A single letter is too *Laverne & Shirley.*"

"Offering monograms on Greene Street in New York is different than on Madison Avenue."

—Andy Spade

ORGANIZING YOUR CLOSET

"Even though I should have a perfectly organized closet, I confess that rearranging everything falls near the bottom of my to-do list. For the most part, though, I keep handbags high and shoes low (and I borrow some real estate from Andy's closet), and I try to keep a separate place for party clothes."

ORGANIZING OPTIONS

BY SEASON—If you have the luxury of space, it's ideal to rotate your clothes seasonally. Not only is this healthier for the clothes (less crowding, for instance), it also makes it easier on you to keep everything neat and sorted.

BY COLOR—If your color bar goes from pink to black, then an arrangement by color lets you select your wardrobe quickly and easily. It also allows for easy upkeep.

BY TYPE—Shirts with shirts, pants with pants, and so forth is pragmatism in motion. As long as you're combining like with like, why not do so by color as well?

HANGING VS FOLDING

Unless the garment is a knit, hanging on padded hangers is best. (Slacks are best hung by the cuffs on trouser hangers.) To keep shirt collars neat and blouses from wrinkling, button the top, middle, and last buttons before putting away. Be sure to do up zippers and empty pockets, too. Sweaters are happiest folded. So are T-shirts, polo shirts, and cotton turtlenecks.

"EVERYTHING IN YOUR CLOSET SHOULD HAVE AN EXPIRATION DATE ON IT THE WAY MILK AND BREAD AND MAGAZINES AND NEWSPAPERS DO."

—ANDY WARHOL

A LIBRARY OF SHOES
(AKA ANDY SPADE'S ORGANIZING PRINCIPLE FOR SHOES)

Acquiring Knowledge—Wallabees

Art & Architecture—Manolo Blahnik, Helmut Lang, Stéphane Kélian, Christian Louboutin, Robert Clergerie

Business—Florsheim, Allen Edmonds, Church's English Shoes, Alden's

Discovery—Sperry Topsiders, Timberland, Sorell boots, scuba socks

Gardening—Wellingtons, rubber clogs

Health—Easy Spirit

Histrionics—Dansko clogs

Humor—Camper, Earth shoes, moon boots, John Fluevog

Leisure—Flip-flops, espadrilles, Jack Rogers, Minnetonka moccasins

Literature—Converse sneakers, Bass Weejuns

Philosophy—Birkenstock, New Balance sneakers

Poetry—Rockport, huaraches

Self-Help—Mephisto

Travel—Clarks Desert Boots

Turning Japanese?—Nike Dunk Low

> "SOCKS ARE FREQUENTLY NOT WORN ON SPORTING OCCASIONS, OR ON SOCIAL OCCASIONS, FOR THAT MATTER. THIS PROVIDES A YEAR-ROUND BEACHSIDE LOOK . . . SO THAT COMFORT MAY BE THROWN ASIDE."
>
> —THE OFFICIAL PREPPY HANDBOOK

SHOE SALVOS

Use shoe trees to keep your shoes in shape. As a backup, try tissue.

To extend the life of your shoes and to make walking more comfortable, ask the shoemaker to add a thin rubber sole (in black or natural).

A light protective spray on your leather shoes will help fortify them against rain, snow, and salt.

Maintenance is the key to the life of any shoe. Be sure to regularly clean and polish your leather shoes, wash your sneakers, and add taps to your toes and heels.

WARDROBE ABCs

"If you go through history, you can tell how people are feeling
about themselves by how they dress. When Andy and I watch movies,
I'm always captivated by how the actress is dressed and what that says
about her character—or what it says about the costume designer."

SOME BASIC CLOTHING DEFINITIONS...

A-LINE SKIRT/DRESS—Usually fitted at the waist, and gradually flares to resemble an "A"
at the hem. The skirt length is just to the knee or slightly above.

BALACLAVA—A knit cap that covers the head and neck. Rudi Gernreich designed an all-over
giraffe-print ensemble, including a balaclava and matching shoes.

BATEAU—A wide, straight neckline, of the same depth front and back; a boat-shaped neckline,
that meets at points on the shoulders. Also known as a boat neck. Think of Brigitte Bardot in
Viva Maria (1965) in her little bateau top.

BOX PLEAT—Two folds of fabric brought together to make a pleat.

BRACELET SLEEVE—Three-quarter-length sleeve that extends below the elbow, about halfway
to the wrist. So named because it's ideal for wearing with bracelets.

CAPRI PANTS—Straight-cut pants that taper at the calf. The ankles are not covered. In *Send Me
No Flowers* (1964), Doris Day is a daisy herself in a yellow chinoiserie top and yellow Capri pants.

EMPIRE WAIST—Originated in the court of Empress Josephine. Typically décolleté with a
high waistline just below the bust, the dress falling straight to the hem.

FISHTAIL HEM—A hem in the shape of a fishtail, having a V-shaped cutout.

FLAT-FRONT PANTS—Straight-cut pants, often with an inset waist and
without pockets. In *High Society* (1956), Grace Kelly wears a buff-colored
blouse with a wide leather belt and tailored slacks. She's sporty and elegant.

GROSGRAIN—A closely woven corded fabric, traditionally made with
silk or rayon, and often with a cotton fill for added strength.

HANDKERCHIEF HEM—Consisting of large or small squares of
cloth draping in gentle folds.

JEWEL-NECK—Similar to the crewneck, but without ribbing, and
often dressier.

KNIFE PLEAT—Narrow folds of fabric that are all turned to one side.

MACKINTOSH—Refers to a British raincoat of a lightweight waterproof rubberized cotton.

MAILLOT—A one-piece bathing suit.

MITT—Woman's gloves that leave the fingers uncovered.

MONOKINI—The topless swimsuit designed by Rudi Gernreich in 1964, which is still considered to be avant-garde.

MOTHER-AND-DAUGHTER FASHIONS—Look-alike dressing was popular in the 1940s and items of clothing were identical save for size. In the 1940s and early 50s, sportswear designer Claire McCardell produced a line of Baby McCardells so that mother and daughter could have matching frocks and swimsuits.

NOTCHED COLLAR—A classic two-piece collar that lays flat and is always worn open.

PALAZZO PANTS—A wide-legged pant, extending from the waist to the floor. Sometimes known as *hostess pants*. In the mid-1960s, Anne Klein designed jumpsuits with palazzo pants, which were ideal for outdoor entertaining.

PATCH POCKET—A piece of material sewn on three edges to the outside of a garment, usually a coat or jacket.

PEPLUM—A small ruffle or flounce extending from the waist of a blouse or jacket, or bottom of a skirt. With Dior's New Look of 1947, the peplum jacket came back into style.

PRINCESS—A close-fitting, slenderizing silhouette that hangs unbroken from the shoulders.

SARONG SKIRT—A long piece of fabric that wraps around the body and is often tied at the side. May be worn alone, or as a swimsuit cover-up. Originally designed by Edith Head for Dorothy Lamour.

SHAWL COLLAR—An attached collar, without a notch, that extends flat around the neck and usually crosses slightly above or just at the waistline. Lauren Bacall wears a shawl collar cashmere sweater in Douglas Sirk's melodrama *Written on the Wind* (1956).

SHEATH DRESS—A form-fitting silhouette that follows the natural curves of a body. Like the straight skirt, a sheath dress neither tapers nor has added fullness at the hem.

STRAIGHT SKIRT—A straight silhouette, without either tapering or gradual fullness.

SUNBURST PLEAT—Like a knife pleat, but the pleats are narrow at the top and widen at the bottom, producing a flared effect. May also be sewn on the bias so that the pleats radiate from the center.

TRENCH COAT—Double-breasted raincoat that has deep pockets and a wide belt. Some have inverted V-pleats on the back or removable linings. Typically khaki or black. In Carol Reed's *The Third Man*, Anna Schmidt as Alida Valli wears a trench coat to keep out the damp Viennese chill.

CLOTHING DETAILS...

BUTTON LOOPS—Fabric sewn into loops for buttons instead of buttonholes.

CONTRAST STITCHING—Deliberately visible stitching that is a different color than the fabric.

FROG CLOSURE—Chinese-style closure of decorative cording or braid. The "button" is a ball made with the cording.

GROMMETS—Reinforced holes, sometimes found on rainwear and on belts and shoes with laces.

PIPING—A thin, contrasting piece of fabric used to outline or accent a dress, slacks, or even pajamas. Functionally, piping covers seams.

TOGGLE—A rod-shaped closure, usually made of leather, cord, or faux horn.

ZIPPER—Next to the button, the most ubiquitous means of closure for clothing. Two facing rows of teeth are pulled together by means of a slider, thereby closing a garment.

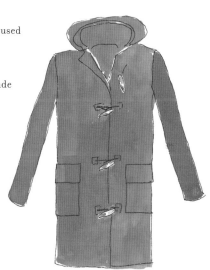

ENDURING STYLE...
THE ZIPPER (1917)

Fashion lore ascribes the invention of the zipper to Elsa Schiaparelli in the 1930s, though it was in fact created by Swedish engineer Gideon Sundback, whose patent for the "Separable Fastener" was issued in 1917. Around that time, the B. F. Goodrich Company used Sundback's zipper on a pair of boots, which they called the Zipper boot. By the 1930s, the zipper had become a suitable closure for women's garments, among them the seductively fitted long gowns of the period. By 1937, the zipper triumphed over the button in "the Battle of the Fly."

PLAIDS, TARTANS, AND TWEEDS

Asking the difference between a plaid and a tartan is a little like asking the difference between a hat and a cap. In the broadest sense, a plaid is a wool or cotton twill based on Scottish tartan patterns. Some of the more familiar plaids include argyle, buffalo plaid, glen plaid, and houndstooth. A tweed, too, is Scottish in origin (the name comes from the Tweed River, separating England and Scotland) but is different from its cousins the plaid and tartan. A tweed is a woven twill, typically in wool, and in a variety of weaves. To us, perhaps the most familiar tweeds are herringbone and houndstooth, also known as dogtooth.

TARTANS

You don't have to be a Scot to take pleasure in the vast world of tartans.

FLOWER—The blues and greens represent the Scottish bluebell and thistle.

IRISH NATIONAL—For all the Irish ex-patriates, from the House of Edgar.

CAROLINA—This historic tartan goes back to c. 1730, and possibly even to 1661, when the pattern was used in the wedding ribbons of Charles II.

TWEEDS

The sturdy tweed will keep you warm through many a blustery and chilly day, even if the only tweed you wear is a herringbone hat.

DELEGATE

CANDACRAIG

MODERN TWEED, inspired by the Glen Guoich

The Harris Tweed label, the trademark of Harris and Lewis, signifies that this soft wool comes from the Hebrides Islands, off the west coast of Scotland.

SOME USEFUL FABRIC TERMS...

ANGORA—May come from either the angora goat or the angora rabbit. A very soft, somewhat fuzzy fiber.

APPLIQUÉ—Refers to a decoration that is sewn or glued onto another fabric.

BOUCLÉ—From the French for "buckled" or "ringed." An uneven yarn that forms loops at intervals. The fabric is usually springy.

CHAMBRAY—A woven fabric (usually cotton) that combines white with colored thread.

CHARMEUSE—A satin weave with a twill back, which is used for evening dresses as well as pajamas.

CHIFFON—A soft, sheer, and airy fabric. The best chiffon is silk, though it may also be made from rayon.

DUPIONI—Although similar to shantung, dupioni fabric has thicker, irregularly sized fibers woven into the fabric.

FAUX FUR—Synthetic fabric instead of real animal fur.

FLANNEL—A soft cotton or wool that has a slight nap on one side and a plain or twill on the back.

GINGHAM—Typically in cotton, woven to create checks or plaids. When two colors are combined the yarns are usually in the same palette. Traditional ginghams are white with a second color.

KNIT—One set of yarns, run in one direction, that are looped.

MADRAS—Part of the gingham family but typically with more colors and more overall pattern. Cotton madras may also come from India.

PAISLEY—A woven or printed wool, cotton, or silk with colorful, botanically inspired curving shapes.

PIQUÉ—Usually made with cotton, but may also be done in silk or rayon. A durable ribbed medium or heavyweight fabric.

SATIN—A lustrous feel and a dull back is the most basic definition of this fabric. Other satins include double-face, duchesse, slipper satin, and peau de soie.

SEERSUCKER—A lightweight fabric having crinkled alternating stripes. Traditionally, seersucker is white with a second color. The word seersucker comes from the Persian *shirushaker*, literally "milk and sugar."

SHANTUNG—A plain weave whose irregular texture results from uneven slubbed yarns. Usually in silk.

SHIRTING STRIPE—A stripe fabric suitable for shirts.

TAFFETA—A smooth fabric (silk, rayon, synthetic) having a sheen.

TERRY—A pile cotton, with loops on both sides. The larger the loop, the greater the absorbency. Turkish towels have a pile on one side only.

VELVET—A silk, cotton, rayon, or synthetic combined with a little worsted having a soft pile surface. The back is usually plain.

AND CLASSICS WE ALL KNOW...
CANVAS

CASHMERE

COTTON

DENIM

LINEN

SILK

WOOL

The Mongolian goat produces the finest cashmere.

GRADING COTTON
EGYPTIAN COTTON—Less consistent in fiber quality than pima; grown in the Nile Valley.

PIMA COTTON—A hybrid of American and Egyptian cottons; grown in Texas.

SEA ISLAND COTTON—The finest cotton; grown off the coast of Georgia.

UPLAND COTTON—The staple of American cotton; grown and used worldwide.

CARING FOR YOUR CLOTHES

SUGGESTIONS FOR YOUR VINTAGE CLOTHES...

Avoid hanging garments on wire hangers. Padded hangers are suitably gentle.

Store sweaters with mothballs or the herbal equivalent.

To clean your clothes, hand-washing with a mild soap is the safest route. If you decide to machine-wash, again use a mild detergent.

The safest way to dry your clothes is to lay them flat.

Clothing with special appliqué, such as beading, sequins, or closures, are wisely sent to a dry cleaner with experience in handling vintage garments.

Use clear nail polish to "mend" small holes in polyester or nylon.

Bleach is not your friend . . . no matter how much you want to brighten old whites. Pretreat with a mild detergent and then wash. You may need to repeat this for best results. The sun is a time-honored brightener, so if you have time and space, hang your whites outdoors to dry.

Reweavers are miracle workers, and usually can mend tiny holes in cashmere, pulled threads, failing seams, drooping sequins.

CLASSIC SIZE GUIDE

If you're a fan of vintage clothes, then you know that a vintage size 6 is like a modern size 8. This chart should help you determine sizes for vintage and more contemporary clothing.

SIZE	2	4	6	8	10	12
BUST	32½"	33½"	34½"	35½"	36½"	38"
WAIST	24"	25"	26"	27"	28"	29½"
HIP	35"	36"	37"	38"	39"	40½"

CARING FOR CASHMERE...

Wash in plenty of lukewarm water with mild detergent or baby shampoo.

Gently squeeze the sweater rather than scrub.

Rinse in several washes of cool water until the water runs clear.

Roll up in a towel to absorb excess moisture.

Lay flat, block, and dry away from excessive heat.

Touch up with a warm iron, with your sweater turned inside-out.

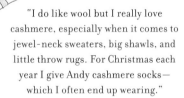

"I do like wool but I really love cashmere, especially when it comes to jewel-neck sweaters, big shawls, and little throw rugs. For Christmas each year I give Andy cashmere socks — which I often end up wearing."

QUALITY CASHMERE

This soft, luxury fiber is among the worthiest indulgences in a wardrobe, for cashmere has the cachet of quality and lasts for years. (For this reason, it's possible to accumulate a cashmere collection over time.) When shopping for cashmere, the most important considerations are density and ply. Look for a sweater that has heft and feels substantial. Many one-ply cashmeres are lovely; two-ply are sublime (three- and four-ply are almost sinful). Summer cashmere has a higher yarn gauge and thus is thinner, making it ideal for wear year-round. But be on the lookout for show-through, which usually indicates a poor-quality weave.

CARING FOR CLOTHING WITH NATURAL FIBERS

Although man-made fibers have resulted in more choices in fabrics, no amount of invention will ever replace the purity and pleasure of natural fibers. Ask yourself: can a bike replace a car? No, but it's nice to own both.

COTTON—You can safely put most cotton clothing in the washing machine and dryer unless the care tag indicates otherwise. Although some cotton garments are preshrunk, if you want to be certain that sleeves don't inch their way up toward your elbows, avoid extremely hot temperatures when washing and drying.

LINEN—Its delicate appearance aside, linen is actually the most durable and long-lasting of the natural fibers. Washing also renews linen's smooth surface, so unless you're dealing with antique linen clothing, most of today's linen can be hand-washed or put in the machine on the gentle cycle. A good rule of thumb is warm water for whites, cool water for colors. Use a mild detergent and be sure to rinse well. For a crisp finish to collars and cuffs, iron linen while slightly damp.

SILK—This luxury fabric requires a bit more care than most fibers, for it stains easily and readily absorbs odor, such as perfume. While some brave souls feel any silk can be hand-washed, for most of us the manufacturer's care tag is the best advice to follow. Ironing a washable silk requires that you use a low setting and work on the reverse side. A press cloth is surprisingly effective.

WOOL—Of all the natural fibers, wool is the warmest of all, even when the surrounding temperature is damp or chilly. (Wool in fact releases heat when in a cool environment.) Wool can actually tolerate a good deal of dirt, which means less frequent washings. However, to keep your sweaters in their best condition after you wear them, they should "rest" for at least a day, preferably on hangers and where there is good air circulation. Sometimes the steam from a shower helps refresh the wool. Dry cleaning is the usual method of cleaning wool, unless the care tag specifies that hand-washing is preferable or acceptable. Whichever method you choose, in general fewer cleanings are better for the life and look of your wool clothes.

INTERNATIONAL LAUNDRY LEXICON

wash   bleach   dry   iron   dryclean

WASHING WHAT YOU WEAR...

Lingerie is best hand-washed with mild soap and
lukewarm water. Treated well, it will last longer, too.

Summer-weight blouses benefit from being washed by hand with mild detergent. After rinsing,
don't wring the blouse but allow it to drain in the sink for about ten minutes. Then hang it on a
plastic hanger and fasten the top, middle, and bottom buttons. Gently smooth the blouse into
shape. Not only will this cut down on wrinkles, the blouse will dry faster, too.

If you choose to wash a wool sweater, gently roll it in a towel to absorb excess moisture. Dry flat.
(Hanging it to dry will not only damage the fibers, but your sweater will "grow" by several inches.)

Hand-washing cashmere sweaters is actually healthy for them, and prevents the residue buildup
from dry cleaning.

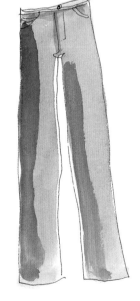

Good socks are a worthy candidate for hand-wash. Air-drying also
prevents stressing more delicate fibers or elastins such as spandex.

To keep your blue jeans *blue* and an ideal fit, wash them inside out
and gently dry.

A CAUTIONARY NOTE
ABOUT DRY CLEANING...

This great time-saver should be used judiciously,
especially when it comes to your sweaters and coats.
Over time, the chemicals can cause colors to fade and the
fabric to weaken. Whites, in particular, age on a fast
track when repeatedly dry-cleaned. Party clothes (lace,
satin, silk chiffon, and those with special sleeves, hems,
and so forth) are best taken to dry-cleaning specialists.

A FEW CLOSING WORDS OF ADVICE...

Do your sweaters pill? The little bits of accumulated wool can be safely trimmed with a simple device
known as a de-fuzzer. (You can find these in notions departments or in home furnishings stores.)

Leave your cat or dog at home when you go out: use a lint roller to remove any stray pet hairs—
especially if you're wearing black.

STAIN CHART

Stains are the gremlins of a woman's wardrobe, and no matter how careful you are, they always seem to turn up. One general rule is to treat a fabric stain with water as hot as you feel the garment can withstand. Keep in mind, too, that sometimes the solution is one that requires multiple efforts. And some stains, in spite of your best efforts, simply won't disappear. But on one point there is universal agreement: the faster a stain is treated, the better the result.

SUBSTANCE	SOLUTION
BERRIES	Soak in cool water. Dab with denatured alcohol and flush with white vinegar. Dab again with some detergent.
CHOCOLATE	Act fast. Use a prewash stain remover and wash as soon as possible. Chocolate is a tough stain to remove and may require more than one try. Even so, don't be surprised if some traces remain.
COFFEE (black or with sugar)	Flush the spot with cool water or with white vinegar; soak for 30 minutes. Spot-treat with detergent.
COFFEE (with milk)	Use a dry-cleaning solvent, and allow to dry. Spot-treat with detergent and then wash in hot water.
INK	BALLPOINT: Place the stain facedown on paper towels and sponge with either rubbing alcohol, some detergent, or dry cleaning solvent. Rinse before laundering. FELT TIP: A multistep process. First, pour hot water over the stain to flush what you can. Repeat if needed. Dry, then work in a little detergent. Rinse. Soak for at least 4 hours in water to which you have added a couple of tablespoons of household ammonia. Rinse. Repeat if needed.
LIPSTICK	Place the stain facedown on paper towels and use either a prewash stain remover or sponge with a dry-cleaning solvent. Rinse. Follow with gentle detergent rubbed into the spot until the stain is gone. Rinse and launder.
TEA	As with chocolate, work fast. To remove the tea discoloration, flush with lemon juice, then follow with a little diluted bleach. Depending on whether the tea had sugar or milk, see instruction for coffee, above.
WINE, red	Treat asap. Cover the stain with salt and leave for 5 minutes. Stretch the stained garment over a bowl or basin, secure with a rubber band, and pour boiling water through it from a distance of at least a foot. Repeat until the stain is gone.
WINE, white.	Treat asap. Flush as needed with cool water. Launder.

JEWELRY

CARING FOR YOUR COSTUME JEWELRY...

"Over the years I have found a hanging bag to be the easiest way to keep my fun jewelry. I can see everything and the bag takes up less room in my closet than all this jewelry would in a drawer."

Avoid wearing your jewelry just after applying PERFUME. Wait a few minutes to allow the scent to set.

The ideal way to store your jewelry is to wrap it in SOFT MUSLIN and tuck it into a plastic bag. (And don't forget to label the bag.) You can also skip the cloth and just use the plastic bag. When possible, store your pieces in an acid-free environment.

Avoid using WATER on any pieces containing an adhesive.

Settings can loosen, so have PRONG SETTINGS checked.

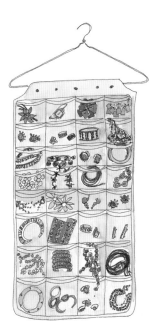

TIPS FOR CLEANING, HANDLING, AND STORING YOUR FINE JEWELRY...

The safest way to clean your washable jewelry is to use a MILD DETERGENT and warm water. (Steer clear of products with ammonia or alcohol.) It may be tempting to use the sink to wash your jewelry, but please don't—a drain is a sure route to loss. Instead, choose a small plastic basin.

What can you WASH?—diamonds, sapphires, and rubies are washable, as are most transparent stones *except* emeralds. Take care to avoid using soap and water on amber, coral, jade, kunzite, lapis lazuli, opal, pearls, and turquoise. If in doubt, consult a jeweler.

PEARLS are delicate (perhaps that's why we love them), so store them separately in pouches to avoid any scratches. Once you own a pearl necklace, take care to have it restrung every couple of years. It's no fun if the string breaks and the pearls scatter! After wearing pearls, it's always a good idea to wipe them with a soft damp cloth, which removes any acid they may have picked up from your skin and helps retain their natural luster.

Don't leave your TORTOISESHELL or ivory in direct sunlight. Tanning is not good for them or for us.

Extreme TEMPERATURES can affect some jewelry, especially any with wood, ivory, or opals.

Separately pouch valuable or beloved pieces, which prevents scratches and tangled chains. Plus, it's an easier way to keep track of everything. A JEWELRY BOX is designed to keep your gems in good condition.

TRAVEL SAFE: keep your jewelry with you when you board a plane, rather than in your checked luggage.

THANK YOU

It seems that every project I venture upon involves the helping hands of many people, and this book is no exception. Everyone has pitched in—from my husband and colleagues at kate spade to my dog, Henry, indispensable bon vivant and critic.

Julia Leach, who oversees our creative department and is a longtime friend of Andy's and mine, has truly shouldered the responsibility of putting this book together. I don't know how she manages to have so much energy and such grace under pressure, but she is a god-send. Working in tandem with Julia is our editor and new friend, Ruth Peltason, whose enthusiasm and expertise has helped all of us make this book special. They were joined in their efforts by Virginia Johnson, our gifted illustrator; designer Alberta Testanero, who gave the project its overall look; and Ana Rogers, who took the vision for this book and brought it to life.

Our business partners, Elyce Arons and Pamela Bell, and I were friends long before we started this company, and they have been greatly supportive of this project. Their suggestions, their own experiences, and those we've shared have all contributed to *Style*. So has the friendship and encouragement extended by Robin Marino, president of kate spade. I'm also grateful to Marybeth Schmitt, who has skillfully navigated our publicity efforts. Also at our office I would like to thank Susan Anthony, Barbara Kolsun, Stacy Van Praagh, Meg Touborg, and everyone in our creative department—Biz Zast , Lawren Howell, Jenifer Ruske, Cheree Berry, Naseem Niaraki, and

Anthony Coombs. Katie Powell Brickman and Elizabeth Yarborough cheerfully provided research.

A book of this nature is somewhat daunting, and I have been "guided" by many women of style whom I admire for their spirit and individual spark, among them Diana Vreeland, Lilly Pulitzer, and Björk. My sincere thanks to the many great costume designers over the years whose films have provided inspiration and instruction. Film critic Carrie Rickey and writer Laura Jacobs have each been a valuable resource, and giving of their time and expertise.

The business of publishing a book is new to me, and I am grateful that our agent, Ira Silverberg, has been so wonderfully wise. I have been fortunate to work with the devoted crew at Simon & Schuster, including David Rosenthal, executive vice president and publisher, whose enthusiasm wowed us all; Amanda Murray, our patient in-house editor; Walter L. Weintz; Michael Selleck; Tracey Guest; and Peter McCulloch. Thank you, thank you.

And then there's my husband, Andy, who first gave me the courage to go into business more than a decade ago and now into books. "We already have so many books and we both love to read," I told him, "do you really think it's a good idea to try being an author?" Well, his answer is before you. Listening to Andy talk about style is an exercise in the less-is-more axiom. His ideas and his infectious spirit and voice are in *Style*, page for page. So, too, is Andy's encouragement, his humor, and his love. I am indeed blessed.

Kate Spade

SELECT BIBLIOGRAPHY

Ballard, Bettina. *In My Fashion: An Intimate Memoir About the People, Places, and Events That Make Up the World of High Fashion.* New York: David McKay Co., 1960.

Bender, Marilyn. *The Beautiful People.* New York: Coward McCann, Inc., 1967.

Benton, Robert, and Harvey Schmidt. *The In and Out Book.* Introduction by Russell Lynes. New York: The Viking Press, 1959.

Bowles, Hamish. *Jacqueline Kennedy: The White House Years: Selections from the John F. Kennedy Library and Museum.* With contributions by Arthur M. Schlesinger, Jr., and Rachel Lambert Mellon. New York: Metropolitan Museum of Art/Bulfinch Press, 2001.

Charles-Roux, Edmond. *Chanel and Her World.* New York: The Vendome Press, 1981.

Dariaux, Geneviève Antoine. *Elegance: A Complete Guide for Every Woman Who Wants to be Well and Properly Dressed on All Occasions.* Garden City, New York: Doubleday & Company, Inc., 1964.

Diamond, Jay and Ellen. *Fashion Apparel and Accessories.* Albany, New York: Delmar Publishers, Inc. 1994.

Esten, John. *Diana Vreeland: Bazaar Years, Including 100 Audacious Why Don't Yous...?* New York: Universe Publishing, 2001.

Gutner, Howard. *Gowns by Adrian: The MGM Years, 1928–1941.* New York: Harry N. Abrams, Inc., Publishers, 2001.

Hawes, Elizabeth. *Fashion is Spinach.* Decorations by Alexey Brodovitch. New York: Random House, 1938.

Head, Edith, and Jane Kesner Ardmore. *The Dress Doctor.* Boston: Little, Brown and Company, 1959.

Head, Edith, and Paddy Calistro. *Edith Head's Hollywood.* Foreword by Bette Davis. New York: E. P. Dutton, Inc. 1983.

Johnson, Anna. *Handbags: The Power of the Purse.* New York: Workman Publishing, 2002.

McDowell, Colin. *Hats: Status, Style, and Glamour.* New York: Thames & Hudson, 1997.

Martin, Richard. *American Ingenuity: Sportswear 1930s–1970s.* New York: The Metropolitan Museum of Art, 1998.

Martin, Richard, and Harold Koda. *Christian Dior.* New York: The Metropolitan Museum of Art/ Harry N. Abrams, Inc., 1996.

——. *Splash! A History of Swimwear.* New York: Rizzoli, 1990.

Mendelson, Cheryl. *Home Comforts: The Art and Science of Keeping House.* New York: Scribner, 1999.

Mendes, Valerie. *Dressed in Black.* New York: V&A Publications in association with Harry N. Abrams, Inc., 1999.

Milbank, Caroline Rennolds. *The Couture Accessory.* New York: Harry N. Abrams, Inc., 2002.

———. *Couture: The Great Designers.* New York: Stewart, Tabori & Chang, Inc., 1985.

O'Keeffe, Linda. *Shoes: A Celebration of Pumps, Sandals, Slippers & More.* New York: Workman Publishing, 1996.

Picken, Mary Brooks. *The Fashion Dictionary: Fabric, Sewing and Dress as Expressed in the Language of Fashion.* New York: Funk & Wagnalls, 1957.

The Portable Dorothy Parker. Introduction by Brendan Gill. Rev. ed. New York: Penguin Books, 1973. Reprint 1977.

Post, Emily. *Etiquette: The Blue Book of Social Usage.* New York: Funk & Wagnalls Co., Publishers, 1945. Reprint 1949.

Rudofsky, Bernard. *Are Clothes Modern?* Chicago: Paul Theobald, 1947.

Snow, Carmel, with Mary Louise Aswell. *The World of Carmel Snow.* New York: McGraw-Hill Book Co., Inc., 1962.

Steele, Valerie, and Laird Borelli. *Handbags: A Lexicon of Style.* New York: Rizzoli Publishers, 1999.

Strunk, William, Jr., and E. B. White. *The Elements of Style.* 2nd ed. New York: The Macmillan Company, 1972.

Tapert, Annette, and Diana Edkins. *The Power of Style: The Women Who Defined the Art of Living Well.* New York: Crown Publishers, Inc., 1994.

Vreeland, Diana, with Christopher Hemphill. *Allure.* Garden City, New York: Doubleday & Co., Inc. 1960.

Warhol, Andy. *Style, Style, Style.* Boston: Bulfinch Press, 1997.

Yohannan, Kohl, and Nancy Nolf. *Claire McCardell: Redefining Modernism.* New York: Harry N. Abrams, Inc., 1998.

ANIMALS WITH STYLE

Morris the cat; Toto; Fala, FDR's Scottie; Black Beauty; Babe; Basket, Gertrude Stein's poodle; Tonto; William Wegman's weimaraners; the countless pugs owned by the Duke and Duchess of Windsor; Asta, the dog star of the *Thin Man* films; Henry.

CARTOON CHARACTERS WITH STYLE

Daisy Duck; Veronica Lodge; Pepe le Pew; Judy Jetson; Snow White; Olive Oyl; Minnie Mouse; Lucy van Pelt; Natasha Fatale; the Pink Panther.

Editors: Ruth A. Peltason, for Bespoke Books
Julia Leach, for kate spade

Designers: Ana Rogers
Alberta Testanero, for kate spade

The author and publisher gratefully acknowledge those writers and designers whose works contributed to this book.

Excerpt from "My Nightmare," by Nora Ephron, in *The New York Times Sunday Magazine,* March 23, 2003

Lyrics from "Fly Me to the Moon," words and music by Bart Howard; TRO—© copyright 1954 (renewed) Hampshire House Publishing Corp., New York, New York

Morris® the Cat © Del Monte Foods

SIMON & SCHUSTER
Rockefeller Center
1230 Avenue of the Americas
New York, NY 10020

SIMON & SCHUSTER and colophon are registered trademarks
of Simon & Schuster, Inc.

For information regarding special discounts for bulk purchases, please contact
Simon & Schuster Special Sales at 1-800-456-6798 or business@simonandschuster.com

Manufactured in Italy

10 9 8 7 6 5 4 3 2 1

Library of Congress Cataloging-in-Publication Data

Spade, Kate.
   Style : always gracious, sometimes irreverent / by Kate Spade ; edited by Ruth Peltason and Julia Leach ; illustrations by Virginia Johnson.
       p. cm.
   Includes bibliographical references.
   1. Clothing and dress. 2. Fashion. 3. Beauty, Personal. 4. Costume—History. I. Peltason, Ruth A. II. Leach, Julia (Julia E.) III. Title.
TT507.S697 2004
391'.2—dc22

                                                                    2003066656

ISBN 0-7432-5067-2